BLUE STAR LINE
AT WAR

1939 - 1945

by

TAFFRAIL

(Captain TAPRELL DORLING, D.S.O., F.R.Hist.S., Royal Navy)

LONDON

W FOULSHAM & CO LTD

NEW YORK TORONTO CAPE TOWN SYDNEY

W. FOULSHAM & CO LTD
Yeovil Road, Slough, Berks, England

ISBN 0-572-00849-X
© Copyright Blue Star Line Ltd. 1973
Printed in Great Britain by
The Camelot Press Ltd, Southampton

BLUE STAR LINE
AT WAR
1939 - 1945

INTRODUCTION

DELVING into the old volumes of Lloyds Register of Shipping in the Admiralty Library, the first mention I could find of the Blue Star Line occurs in the issue for 1912-13, at which time the Company owned four ships ; but actually they commenced operations in 1911 with three ships. In 1916-17, during the First World War, it had 12 vessels, all of their names starting with " Brod." It was in 1920 that the now familiar " Stars " began to appear, in the shape of the *Albion Star* and *Royal Star*, in a total Blue Star fleet of 15 ships.

In the early part of its career the Company's fleet consisted entirely of refrigerated cargo ships voyaging in the main to China and South America. In 1926, however, the Blue Star Line turned its attention to the passenger side of the business, and within a year had established a regular mail and cargo service to South America. Five twin-screw, 16-knot, turbine passenger liners of 14,000 to 15,000 gross tons, and four 11,000 ton, 15-knot refrigerated cargo ships were added to the fleet in about 12 months. The passenger liners, all of which had large refrigerated capacity, were the *Almeda Star*, *Andalucia Star*, *Arandora Star*, *Avelona Star* and *Avila Star ;* and the cargo ships the *Afric Star*, *Napier Star*, *Rodney Star* and *Stuart Star*.

It was not long before the *Arandora Star*, painted white with a red riband and popularly known as " the chocolate box," was transformed into a cruising liner pure and simple, to become a favourite ship with the travelling public during her cruises to Norway, the Baltic, Mediterranean and West Indies.

In the 12 years or so before the Second World War, Blue Star ships, all of them carrying ordinary cargoes outward and for the greater part refrigerated cargoes home, were voyaging regularly to and fro between the United Kingdom, the Continent, North and South America, Canada, South and East Africa, Australia, New Zealand and many ports in the Straits Settlements and the Far East. Thus it was that when war became imminent towards the end of August, 1939, Blue Star ships were scattered all over the world—in Australian waters and the Pacific ; on passage in the Indian Ocean and in the North and South Atlantic ; in port in London, Liverpool, Glasgow, Newcastle-on-Tyne, Dakar, Trinidad, Brisbane and Seattle.

On Monday, August 28th, 1939, the Admiralty broadcast a message to all British merchant ships ordering them to comply with any sailing or routeing instructions that might be issued by the Naval Authorities. Navigation lights must be dimmed, and no other lights must be shown at sea. Restrictions were imposed as to the use of wireless. For the space of the next six years darkness and wireless silence were to be imposed upon British ships except in cases of operational necessity.

One wonders how many British seamen in the outer oceans heard Mr. Neville Chamberlain's message broadcast at 11.15 a.m. on that fateful Sunday, September 3rd, 1939, and what were their feelings as they listened. The Prime Minister said :

> " Consequently this country is at war with Germany. . . . And now that we have resolved to finish it, I know you will all play your parts with calmness and courage. . . . It is of vital importance that you should carry on with your jobs. . . . It is the evil things we shall be fighting against— brute force, bad faith, injustices, oppression and persecution—and against them I am certain the right will prevail."

It did ; but at what a sacrifice !

By the outbreak of war the Blue Star fleet had grown to one of 38 ships of a total of 381,000 gross tons. During the nearly six years of hostilities it lost 29 of its vessels, including all its passenger liners. Ships may be replaced ; but men cannot. And of the Blue Star personnel 646 gave their lives, this number including 11 captains, 47 navigating officers and 88 engineers— these, out of the total of about 30,000 Merchant Navy casualties caused by enemy action during the war.

For most of this multitude the sea is their only sepulchre, and the foaming whitecaps their tombstones. Their epitaphs are written across the sky in the faint smoke-trails of passing steamers. But these merchant seamen were warriors, who died that Britain might live. There never was a " phoney " war at sea. The two Sea Services were engaged from the very beginning. In war the Merchant and the Royal Navies have ever been interdependent and indivisible, the one to carry and the other to protect the food and supplies without which we perish. That fact should be realized by all of us after two great maritime wars in 30 years during which we only survived by a hair's breadth.

On both occasions we narrowly escaped defeat at the hands of the U-boats. In the First World War the year 1917 was the critical one, and April 19th, when 11 British merchantmen were sunk by submarines, the worst day of the blackest month in the war at sea. One out of every four merchant ships that sailed from Great Britain in that April never returned. The year 1942 was the crucial period of the last war, and June the worst month, when Allied losses in merchant ships mounted to the huge total of 135 vessels of 680,000 tons sunk by U-boats out of a total of 160 ships of 800,000 tons destroyed by all causes combined.

In the First World War, which lasted 51 months, submarines sank 4,837 British, Allied and neutral merchant vessels of 11,135,000 tons, with a monthly average of 95 sinkings. In the 68 months of the Second World War during which the battle raged in the Atlantic, U-boats destroyed 2,775 British, Allied and neutral merchant ships of about 14½ million gross tons out of the total loss of 4,786 vessels of more than 21 million gross tons. The average monthly tonnage sunk by U-boats in both wars was roughly the same at about 215,000 gross tons, the disparity in the number of ships being accounted for by the fact that in 1914-18 the average tonnage of vessels sunk was 2,300, whereas by 1939-45 it had increased to 4,400.

The circumstances of the Second World War at sea were infinitely more terrible than in 1914-18. In 1939-45 58 per cent. of all the merchant ship losses were inflicted by U-boats. Enemy aircraft, which did not become a really serious menace until the German occupation of Norway and France, accounted for another 16 per cent. of the shipping losses ; mines for 11 per cent. ; surface vessels for another 7 per cent. ; and unknown causes and the usual hazards of wartime navigation for 8 per cent. While we are upon figures, it is also interesting to note that 53 per cent. of the shipping losses through all causes occurred in the North and South Atlantic, while 54 per cent. of the total losses in all areas—2,562 merchant ships of more than 11¼ million gross tons—were British.

After the fall of France in June, 1940, Britain fought practically single-handed with Germany in control of the western seaboard of Europe from the North Cape to the Franco-Spanish frontier, which provided her with ample bases for U-boats and aircraft.

Italy's entry into the war in the same month vastly increased our commitments in the Mediterranean, while also necessitating the despatch of troops and supply convoys to Egypt round the Cape of Good Hope. With the participation of Japan in the war in December, 1941, our responsibilities became extended to every ocean in the World, and our shipping and the means of protecting it were stretched almost to breaking point. Our new ally, the United States, had yet to get into her stride.

The victory at sea upon which all else depended could not be ascribed to any single service or arm. But we British should realize that a debt we can never repay is due to the men of the Merchant Navies, who, true to their fine tradition, and with a steadfast courage, devotion and endurance, refused to be intimidated by the heavy toll of sinkings, and the threat of their ships being sunk or blown to pieces. If they had failed, the result would not merely have been the defeat of Britain and the disruption of the British Empire ; but the eventual Axis domination of the world.

This book does not pretend to be a history. It is the war story of some of the ships of a single steamship Company, the Blue Star Line, and has been pieced together from various sources, mainly from the narratives of some of those who took part in the incidents I shall describe, and any other information I have been able to secure. The material available is sparse enough. Seamen are proverbially men of few words, and are not much given to spreading themselves on paper. Added to this, wartime regulations forbade the keeping of diaries or the writing of detailed personal letters describing events and movements. After the first few months of the war, too, the necessary censorship prevented the mention of ship losses in the newspapers, while the blitz upon London and other places resulted in the destruction of valuable records. So taking it all in all the collection of material has not been easy.

But this war record of the Blue Star Line, incomplete and scrappy though it may be, is a story of gallantry, endurance, fine seamanship and devotion to duty on the part of Merchant Seamen. Nobody can read the accounts of those hard-fought convoys to Malta ; of an escape from Singapore in the full fury of the Japanese air attacks ; of the various voyages in open boats after ships had been sunk ; and of the cool bravery of officers and men in many differing circumstances of great peril and hardship, without a thrill of pride and admiration for the conduct and hardihood of those who fought the war at sea.

Sea Power, let it be remembered, works in many different ways, and is built up not merely in warships ; but in merchant ships as well. Merchant Seamen were no mere transporters of men, food, munitions of war and material of every sort and kind. They were fighting seamen giving the same service as, and sometimes enduring greater risks and hardships than, their brethren in many of the warships.

Those of us who saw something of the men and the ships of the Merchant Navy during the war, will echo the words of Admiral Sir Neville Syfret. Referring to the merchant ships after one of the convoys to Malta from the west, he wrote in his report :

" The steadfast way in which these ships pressed on their way to Malta, through all attacks, answering every manoeuvring order like a well-trained fleet unit, was a most inspiring sight. . . . The memory of their conduct will remain an inspiration to all who were privileged to serve with them."

TAFFRAIL.

CHAPTER I

THE GERMAN WAR PLAN

THOUGH it may not be strictly germane to the war history of the Blue Star Line, it is interesting briefly to trace the growth and development of the German Navy under the Nazi regime, and to say something of the German ideas of war at sea with Great Britain as her enemy.

In October 1933, about eight months after Hitler's accession to power, Germany withdrew from the International Disarmament Conference and the League of Nations. In 1935, the Nazi Government decided to take the first open steps to free itself from its obligations under the Treaty of Versailles. On March 10th, 1935, Goering announced that Germany was creating a military air force. Six days later a law was passed instituting compulsory military service and fixing the establishment of the German Army at a peacetime strength of 500,000 men. At the same time that the economic preparation for war was being carried out, the German armed forces themselves were preparing for a rebuilding of Germany's armed strength.

To quote the printed judgment* of the trial of the German major war criminals at Nuremberg :

"The German Navy was particularly active in this regard. The official German naval historians, Assmann and Gladisch, admit that the Treaty of Versailles had only been in force for a few months before it was violated, particularly in the construction of a new submarine arm. The publications of Captain Schuessler and Osbert Scherf, both of which were sponsored by the defendant Raeder,† were designed to show the German people the nature of the Navy's effort to re-arm in defiance of the Treaty of Versailles."

*His Majesty's Stationery Office. Cmd. 6964. Miscellaneous No. 12 (1946).

†Admiral Raeder became Chief of Naval Command in 1928 ; and in 1935, under Hitler, Oberbefehlshaber der Kriegsmarine, i.e. Commander-in-Chief of the German Navy. In 1939 he was promoted to Gross-Admiral (Admiral of the Fleet). He was a member of the Reich Defence Council until, on January 30th, 1943, he retired and became Admiral Inspector of the Navy, a purely nominal title. He was replaced by Admiral Doenitz, a submarine officer of the First World War, who in 1935 had been appointed to the command of the first U-boat flotilla commissioned since 1918. In 1936 he became commander of the submarine arm, and was promoted to Vice-Admiral in 1940, and Admiral in 1942.

The rebuilding of the German Navy from 1933 onwards was governed almost entirely by the output of the German ship-building yards and the character of the war of aggression to be waged at sea against Britain. Our London Naval Treaty of 1935, with Germany, *faute de mieux*, allowed her to build up to 35 per cent. of our tonnage in surface warships, and 100 per cent. in submarines. The limitations of the German yards and factories gave the Nazis no hope of building up to this strength until 1944.

In naval matters, as in others, the Germans cheated with great ingenuity and diligence. For instance, the displacements of their capital ships, which had to be made public, were falsified by at least 20 per cent. In the case of the U-boats the official German naval historians had the opportunity to write :

" It is probably in the sphere of submarine construction that Germany adhered the least to the restrictions of the German-British Treaty."

The character of the intended war at sea against England was the subject of considerable dissension in the Nazi hierarchy. Goering, with supreme faith in his Luftwaffe, which he boasted was more than a match for any ships, regarded large sums spent on the Navy as waste of money and effort. Hitler, to some extent, was swayed to his opinion. In general, the High Command was essentially " land minded " and ignorant of the importance and application of sea power. Nevertheless, the Fuehrer supported Raeder's pre-war plans and encouraged the building of a surface fleet and the development of the U-boat arm.

I

In deciding what ships to build, and when, guided by Hitler's conviction that war against Britain could be put off until 1944 or 1945, the building programme was several times altered by Raeder. But in February, 1939, the " ' Z ' Plan," as it was called, allowed for a fleet of 13 battleships, 33 cruisers, four aircraft-carriers, 267 U-boats and a large number of destroyers by about 1946.

However, the increasing tension in 1939 made it clear that war with Britain would come much earlier than 1944. Hitler appreciated the unpreparedness of the German Army for a war of unlimited aggression ; but fearing the rearmament of other nations he decided to strike in 1939.

This meant a complete revision of the German naval plans, and Raeder was forced to postpone his scheme for a properly balanced fleet. Instead, he had to build quickly a fleet capable of dealing sharp offensive blows against British sea communications, in short, a war against merchant shipping. In the spring of 1939 first priority was given to battleships and U-boats. When war became imminent in August the work on new battleships was postponed and submarine production was ordered to be speeded up from 20 to 30 new U-boats a month.

At the same time Raeder fully understood the value of powerful surface ships like the *Scharnhorst, Gneisenau, Bismarck, Tirpitz* ; the three pocket battleships *Admiral Graf Spee, Admiral Scheer* and *Deutschland*, later renamed *Luetzow* ; and the heavy cruisers *Hipper, Bluecher* and *Prinz Eugen*, acting independently against lightly defended convoys. Their presence would mean a heavy strain on the British Fleet, which would have to provide increased protection for all of the convoys, with a consequent decrease in the number of convoys at sea. This, the Germans argued, would affect the flow of supplies to Britain almost as effectually as actual attacks on the convoys themselves.

On September 1st, 1939, Admiral Doenitz, Flag Officer in charge of the U-boats, wrote in an official memorandum :

" The Navy's principal task in the war is the struggle against England, and the one and only possibility of bringing England to her knees with the forces of our Navy, lies in attacking her sea communications in the Atlantic. So long as we do not have sufficient numbers of surface forces which are suitable for this task, it will fall chiefly to the U-boat arm. . . . I believe that the U-boat will always be the backbone of warfare against England, and of the political pressure upon her."

Doenitz went on to write that in all some 300 operational U-boats were necessary, of which about 90 were required simultaneously in the most important area, i.e., in the Atlantic north of the Equator. He pointed out that Germany had no more than 57 U-boats in commission.

Raeder also viewed the prospect of war with Great Britain with dismal forebodings. Writing on September 3rd, 1939, he said :

" Today the war against England and France broke out, the war which, according to the Fuehrer's previous assertions, we had no need to expect before about 1944. The Fuehrer believed up to the last minute that it could be avoided, even if this meant postponing a final settlement of the Polish question."

After summarizing the strength of the German fleet as it

THE RT. HON. WILLIAM, FIRST BARON
VESTEY 1859 – 1940

SIR EDMUND VESTEY, Baronet
1866 – 1953

Founders of the Blue Star Line

might have been in 1944-45, and what help might also have been expected at sea from Italy and Japan, Raeder continued :

" On September 3rd, 1939, Germany entered into a war with Great Britain, as the latter—contrary to the Fuehrer's assumption that ' England did not *need* to fight on account of the Polish question '—thought it expedient to fight now with the Polish question as a pretext. Sooner or later, as she saw it, she would *have* to fight Germany, and then probably under unfavourable military conditions, i.e., against an expanded German Fleet."

Whatever qualms may have been felt by Raeder and Doenitz the die was cast. Between August 19th and 21st 21 U-boats had been sent to take up offensive positions round the British Isles, while on August 21st and 24th, respectively, the pocket battleships *Admiral Graf Spee* and *Deutschland*, with their supply ships *Altmark* and *Westerwald* were sent to their waiting positions in the Atlantic.

The depredations of the surface raiders, with those of the U-boats, were very soon to begin.

2

If Raeder and Doenitz had cause to complain that the German Navy was ill-prepared for war in 1939, Britain was hardly better off. It is true that a measure of rearmament had been started in 1935 ; but for many years before that, and for reasons that are now ancient history, the fighting services had been whittled to the bone. Whereas a Navy or an Air Force can be reduced more or less by a stroke of the pen, they cannot be built up again in four years.

As regards the Navy, we had neglected to replace our older capital ships, which meant, in practice, that the only ships really capable of dealing with the fast and widely mobile German " pocket battleships " in the open oceans were the French battle-cruisers *Dunkerque* and *Strasbourg*. We were short of modern cruisers, and woefully lacking in long-range convoy escorts.

Our escort forces at the outbreak of war consisted of 81 old destroyers, 39 sloops, and nine corvettes. We possessed some 200 vessels of all types, mostly trawlers, fitted with Asdics for the underwater detection of submarines, though few of them could be used for ocean convoy. Until the very end of the war, and in spite of our heavy building programmes, the number of destroyers and escort vessels was never really equal to the demand,

Our losses during hostilities were consistently heavy : destroyers, not all of which were used for convoy or anti-submarine work, 139 ; sloops and frigates, 21 ; corvettes, 28 ; trawlers, 251. At the peak period in 1944 there were under the operational control of the Admiralty no fewer than 880 ships of the British, Dominion and Allied Navies employed on ocean convoy, and about 2,200 vessels of various sorts fitted with Asdics used for anti-submarine and work closer inshore. And still they were insufficient for a convoy system which, at the height of the war against the Axis, embraced every ocean in the world.

By 1939, so far as our lamentably shorn Navy Estimates would permit, Britain had used the breathing-space to develop and perfect anti-submarine tactics, weapons and devices, as well as to build a few escort and anti-submarine vessels and to organize a convoy system. This was the beginning of the huge anti-submarine branch of the Royal Navy which came into being during the war.

As was the case with the Navy, the Air Estimates had also been drastically cut. In 1939 aircraft specially fitted for anti-submarine work were hardly in the picture. The Royal Air Force was desperately short of aircraft. While the Germans had been building numbers of long-range aircraft capable of operating over the ocean, Coastal Command, in its nineteen squadrons, had a number of obsolescent aircraft of low en-durance which had nothing more than small bombs with which to attack submarines. Anti-submarine exercises had been carried out before the war, though never on the scale they deserved. The striking power of those well-equipped, long-range squadrons, which, thanks to the introduction of radar and the vast improvements in, and development of, anti-submarine weapons, were later to harass and to sink the U-boats in mid-ocean and thereby to tip the scale in our favour, had not been fully foreseen.

The first ocean convoys from the Port of London and Liverpool sailed on September 6th and 7th, 1939. Homeward bound convoys from Freetown, Sierra Leone, started a week later, and from Jamaica, Halifax and Gibraltar, respectively, on September 15th, 19th and 26th.

In those early days the escorts, short in numbers and much

overworked, usually took the outward-bound convoys no more than 200 miles out into the Atlantic, after which the merchant ships dispersed to their several destinations. The escorts then steamed to a rendezvous, met an incoming convoy, usually accompanied by one of the older battleships or a cruiser as a protection against surface raiders, and brought it home. This system was coupled with " evasive routeing," by which convoys were diverted clear of known or suspected U-boat concentrations. Closer to the British Isles the homeward and outward-bound convoys had the additional protection of trawlers and other craft fitted with Asdics and depth-charges, and what few aircraft were available. But the deep-water convoys were desperately short of escorts. In January, 1940, I was at sea in the Atlantic with a 7½ knot convoy of more than 50 ships, for which the escort consisted of one old destroyer and one sloop.

Later, as the U-boats started to operate further and further afield, the escorts accompanied their convoys for greater distances into the Atlantic. But the lot of the escort commanders was difficult indeed. The problems of how best to use their small forces in hunting a submarine, rescuing survivors, whipping in stragglers, and guarding against further attack, strained their ingenuity and endurance almost to breaking point in one of the most inhospitable and boisterous oceans in the world.

By April, 1941, the U-boats were operating within 500 miles of the Canadian coast. To meet this new menace escorting groups and aircraft of Coastal Command were stationed in Iceland, their duty being to cover the convoys to the neighbourhood of Greenland from the point to the southward where the escorts from the United Kingdom had to turn back to refuel. Very few of the destroyer escorts had sufficient endurance to cross the Atlantic and to hunt U-boats on the way. The relay system of convoy was uneconomic. Moreover, it left a considerable gap in mid-ocean which could not be covered by aircraft from either Britain, Iceland or Canada.

The months of April and May, 1943, will probably be chosen by future historians as the turning point of the U-boat war, and the critical period when the offensive at sea passed into the hands of the Allies. With the advent of the new frigates with long endurance " end to end " convoy across the Atlantic had at last become possible. More and more British, Canadian and American very long-range aircraft were also becoming available to close the gap south of Greenland, while their efforts were supplemented by aircraft of the Naval Air Arm flown from escort carriers working with the convoys. Independent support groups of surface vessels, untrammelled by having to guard the convoys, were also hunting the U-boats wherever they might be found.

It cannot too often be stressed that throughout the war the North Atlantic was the vital area in which the bulk of our convoy escorts had to be concentrated. It was there that the convoys of merchant ships were gathered in strength bringing home the supplies upon which our very existence depended. If that supply line were cut Britain was doomed.

Criticism was sometimes heard because certain of the faster ships sailed unescorted in the more remote areas like the South Atlantic. However, with our heavy commitments in the North Atlantic ; the troop and supply convoys to the Middle East round the Cape of Good Hope ; not to mention the convoys to Malta and those supplying the Allied Army in North Africa after November, 1942 ; with the extra drain upon our resources by having to send large naval forces into the Indian Ocean and Pacific after Japan's entry into the war, it was physically impossible to provide escorts for each and every vessel. The escorts simply did not exist.

Moreover, the speed of a convoy is always the speed of its slowest ship, and to have linked fast ships to slow convoys, except, of course in the most highly dangerous areas, would not greatly have reduced the risks. We should not have been making the best use of our shipping, and it would have resulted in delay in the delivery of all-important cargoes, and further congestion at the British terminal ports which were already under heavy attack by bombing.

Taking all the circumstances into consideration, particularly our unpreparedness in the numbers of escort craft and aircraft available for the defence of trade at the outbreak of war, our convoy system was organized and run with consummate skill, and, in spite of the inevitable vicissitudes of war, ended by being a triumphant success.

One cannot minimize the losses ; but for each ship that was sunk there were many more that got through in safety.

CHAPTER II

I

DORIC STAR
December 2nd, 1939

ON the outbreak of war on September 3rd, 1939, the 5,600 ton steamer *Ionic Star*, completed in 1917, lay at Rio de Janeiro. Wrecked in the Irish Sea on October 17th, she was the first war loss sustained by the Blue Star Line.

When war was declared the *Doric Star*, a 12-knot, 10,000 ton steamer built in 1921 and commanded by Captain William Stubbs, was on passage from the Panama Canal to Auckland, New Zealand. Laden with a full refrigerated cargo of mutton, lamb, cheese and butter from New Zealand and Australia, with a quantity of wool in bales in the 'tween decks, she sailed for England by way of the Indian Ocean and the Cape of Good Hope. Noon on December 2nd, 1939, found her in the South Atlantic on her way home some 1,200 miles from the Cape of Good Hope and 660 miles roughly East by South of St. Helena.

Two months previously, actually on October 1st, the Admiralty had passed a message to all British merchant ships at sea warning them that a German raider might be operating off the east coast of South America. This was the result of the British Steamer *Clement*, of the Booth Line, having been sunk 75 miles south-east of Pernambuco, Brazil, on September 30th. The next day American press reports announced that one of the *Clement's* lifeboats had been picked up by a Brazilian coasting steamer, and that another had come ashore at Maceio, south of Pernambuco. The captain and chief engineer, it was stated, had been taken on board the raider, which, as we know now, was the pocket-battleship *Admiral Graf Spee*.

Having thus advertised herself the *Graf Spee* steamed east, and during October sank four more British ships on the trade route to the Cape. Their officers and crews were made prisoners, the bulk of them being transferred to the notorious *Altmark*, with which the *Graf Spee* was working. The last of that batch of sinkings, the *Trevanion*, was on October 22nd, not far from St. Helena.

Thereafter the *Graf Spee* disappeared until November 15th, when, having cruised for a time east of the Cape of Good Hope without success, she broke north and sank the small tanker *Africa Shell* at the southern end of the Mozambique Channel. The captain was made a prisoner ; but the rest of the *Africa Shell's* crew were allowed to make for the shore in their boats. It was on November 16th that the warning went forth that an enemy raider was at large in the Indian Ocean. On this same day the *Graf Spee* held up and released the Dutch cargo liner *Mapia* to the southward of Madagascar. Again the raider's captain, Langsdorf, must have known that these incidents would soon be reported. No doubt he hoped the news would cause a still further dispersal of the Allied naval forces already carrying on the hunt in the South Atlantic. Accordingly, he doubled back into the South Atlantic, and on November 28th met the *Altmark* in that lonely part of the ocean near Tristan da Cunha, and replenished his oil fuel and stores. All captains, chief officers, second officers, chief and second engineers, and radio officers were transferred from the *Altmark* to the *Graf Spee* by motor launch.

On December 2nd, homeward bound from the Cape, Captain Stubbs and the officers of the *Doric Star* must have known that one or more raiders were operating. All the same, it cannot have been anything but a very unwelcome surprise when at about 1.0 p.m. on that calm afternoon with its long ocean swell, a heavy shell splashed into the sea and exploded within 100 yards of the *Doric Star*. " A couple of minutes later a vessel was sighted about a point on the port quarter," Captain Stubbs wrote later.

" At about 1.10 p.m. a second shell exploded within 200 yards off the starboard bow, and the overtaking vessel was seen to be a battleship."

Those shells were fired at extreme range, before the *Graf Spee's* hull was visible. What Captain Stubbs saw was the top of her tall control tower showing over the clear-cut rim of the horizon.

Some of the prisoners in the *Graf Spee* lived in a small central room immediately beneath the aeroplane. They had heard the 'plane catapulted off, and the pilot, apparently, had first sighted the *Doric Star* and reported back by wireless.

" After first sighting the vessel," Captain Stubbs continues, " I ordered the Wireless Operator (Mr. William Comber) to transmit the raider distress call, also signalled the engine-room for all possible speed. After the second shot I realised it was impossible to escape, so stopped the engines and ordered the wireless operator to amplify the message and state battleship attacking. By this time I could read the daylight morse lamp from battleship signalling ' Stop your wireless,' but I took no notice of this signal. As the battleship approached I gave orders to the engine-room to stand by for scuttling, and as it appeared that our distress call had not been heard I ordered Chief Engineer (Mr. W. Ray) to start and scuttle. A few minutes later the wireless operator reported that our message had been repeated by another British vessel and also a Greek vessel, so I countermanded the orders for scuttling, then threw overboard all confidential papers and books, breech of gun, ammunition and rifles, also all papers about cargo. After distress call had been transmitted I ordered the wireless operator to cease transmitting, as the battleship was exhibiting a notice—' Stop your wireless or I will open fire.' The *Doric Star*, a 12-knot ship with one anti-submarine gun right aft, had no alternative but to obey."

The *Graf Spee* lowered a fast motor-boat, and the British ship was boarded by a party of three officers and about 30 men. They dispersed to various parts of the ship with drawn revolvers—the bridge, the wireless room and engine-room. The captain was taken to his cabin and questioned, while every hole and corner was closely examined. The wireless room was searched for codes and cyphers, and the radio officer asked if he had sent out his position, to which he replied that of course he had. Asked about his cargo, Captain Stubbs replied that he carried only wool, whereupon the *Doric Star's* crew were ordered to remove the hatch covers of two of the holds. The Germans, simpler than usual, saw only bales of wool in the 'tween decks and were satisfied. (Great was their fury, hours after the *Doric Star* had been sunk by gunfire and a torpedo, when they discovered she had carried more than 8,000 tons of refrigerated meat, butter and cheese, just the things they most urgently needed after more than 100 days at sea.)

The crew were given ten minutes to collect lifebelts, blankets, eating utensils and any effects they could carry, and were then transferred to the *Admiral Graf Spee* in the launch. Like other ships, the *Doric Star* appears to have been looted of instruments like sextants, chronometers, binoculars, telescopes and even typewriters. One British captain, who had tried to keep his presentation sextant, was roughly informed it was confiscated by the Reich. He was given a receipt for it, as well as for his ship. As for the sextant, no doubt Mr. Churchill would pay for another.

Just before he left the *Doric Star* Captain Stubbs saw three or four bombs exploded over the starboard side. These did not sink her, for an hour later the *Admiral Graf Spee* fired seven 5·9 in. shell into her, and finally sent her to the bottom with a torpedo.

The Shaw, Savill and Albion Company's 8,000 ton steamer *Tairoa* was intercepted at 6.0 a.m. next morning, December 3rd, about 170 miles south-west of where the *Doric Star* had been sunk. The prisoners on board the *Graf Spee*, who now included all the officers and men from the *Doric Star*, first heard the alarm buzzer calling the Germans to action stations, and then the reports of what sounded like 5·9 inch guns. Next came the " pom-pom-pom " of a heavy machine gun, followed after about an hour by another series of heavy shots. As one of the prisoners—Mr. A. H. Brown, chief officer of the *Huntsman*—relates : " We heard later that six shots from 5·9 inch guns and finally a torpedo were fired to sink the *Tairoa*. At about 9.0 a.m. the captain and some of the officers from this steamer arrived in our room. The early firing had been to stop the radio, but the operator had gone on sending until his machine was eventually hit, though he himself escaped injury. Five of the *Tairoa's* crew were wounded, three deck-boys sufficiently to be detained in hospital on the warship for a week. We were now 51 in one small room. Packed, without room to sit, we ate our meals in relays."

The room measured 17 x 20 feet, with a small pantry and lavatory with 11 washing bowls attached. The food, which was largely synthetic, was not much to boast about, though it was said to have been the same as that served out to the German crew. Bitterly did the latter regret the frozen meat, cheese, butter and eggs so hastily sunk in the *Doric Star*. One hears that the German boarding officer incurred the severe displeasure of his captain.

In all, there were now 196 prisoners on board the *Graf Spee*, the crews of the *Doric Star* and *Tairoa* being locked up in a compartment further aft. The congestion, however, was relieved on December 6th, when the *Graf Spee* again met the *Altmark* and most of the prisoners were removed to her. There were now 29 in the officers room, which included the captains, chief officers, chief engineers, chief refrigerating engineers, radio officers and one passenger. Among them were Captain Stubbs, Chief Officer S. Ransom, Radio Officer W. Comber, Chief Engineer W. Ray, and Chief Refrigerating Engineer J. C. Hulton, all of the *Doric Star*.

The prisoners were reinforced the next evening when the British steamer *Streonshalh* was sunk by gunfire. As Mr. Brown says—

" We now knew we were on the South American shipping routes. We now had thirty-one prisoners in our room, and thirty, the *Streonshalh's* crew, in a room forward. The three wounded were in our room."

For four days, the *Graf Spee* steamed south-westward towards the River Plate. At dawn each day, and again in the evening, the prisoners heard the raider's 'plane catapulted off. It sighted nothing. The routine for the captives was monotonous enough. Hammocks were passed into the officers' room at 9.0 each night, and as soon as everyone was turned in the guard put out the lights. Called at 6.30 a.m., hammocks had to be lashed up and passed outside, after which chairs were passed in. Hot and cold water was available in the lavatory from 6.30 to 7.30 a.m., after which it was shut off until evening. The dreary breakfast came at seven o'clock, followed by an hour's exercise on deck from eight to nine. Dinner came at 11.0 a.m. and tea at 4.0 p.m., with another hour's exercise from five to six. The compartment had no portholes ; but skylights overhead. The prisoners had two packs of cards and a few of the library books taken from sunken ships. In those two crowded compartments life was wearisome indeed ; but it was " heaven," as someone said, to the existence in the notorious *Altmark*.

Then came December 13th, and at daylight the aeroplane overhead was 'revved up as usual. Before it could be catapulted off, however, the prisoners heard the urgent alarm signals. The door to their compartment was screwed down and locked, the skylight closed and the steel covers screwed down overall. After a short pause heavy firing began and continued. The prisoners soon guessed the *Graf Spee* was up against something different to an unarmed merchantman. They could feel the vibration of the ship at high speed, and her heeling over under full helm. She shook heavily at times, though they were unable to tell whether the thudding impacts were caused by the raider's own guns or the impact of shell striking her.

The *Graf Spee* was in contact with Commodore Harwood's three cruisers, *Ajax*, *Achilles* and *Exeter*. It is unnecessary here to describe the battle of the River Plate ; but as one of the British captains aboard the *Graf Spee* said—

"You can imagine our feelings when we felt the shuddering blows of shells striking the ship. We knew it was the intention of the attacking ship to blow our temporary home out of the water. We felt that if she succeeded in doing so it would be for the good of the country, and every time a shot hit us we all said, 'Well hit, sir ! That was a good one.' But we felt like rats in a trap shut up in our tiny compartment of twenty feet by seventeen."

The first definite knowledge they had of direct hits was at about 7.30 a.m., when a shell burst over the officers compartment, putting out all the lights except one. The deck overhead was driven down and the fore and aft supporting beam fractured, while one of the skylight covers was carried away and the skylight smashed. Some shell fragments fell into the room ; but nobody was hurt.

Heavy firing continued until nearly nine o'clock. Watching the ammunition parties in turn through a small screw hole in the door, the prisoners saw the Germans looked very concerned and glum. Many killed and wounded were carried past during a lull in the action, and some of the Germans were physically sick. Most of the *Graf Spee's* crew were lads of between 17 and 22, with a small sprinkling of older men. Some of the youngest had never been to sea before, and had been sent off after a few month's training ashore. Hit 27 times, the *Graf Spee* had 36 killed and about 60 wounded.

Nobody came to see if any of the prisoners were wounded until nearly eleven o'clock, when a German officer outside shouted to ask if they were all right. They replied that they were and wanted some coffee. None was available, for British shell had demolished the galleys, bakeries and provision rooms. After about half-an-hour's delay a " dixie " full of limejuice and water, with four loaves of black bread, were passed into the room and the door locked again.

The *Exeter*, badly damaged and on fire, with all her guns out of action and a loss of 61 killed and 23 wounded, had disappeared to the south-east at slow speed, doing all she could to repair the damage and make herself seaworthy. But all through the rest of the morning and afternoon the *Graf Spee* was shadowed by the *Ajax* and *Achilles*. Both ships had expended a great amount of ammunition, and now that the *Exeter* had gone, Commodore Harwood could not risk further prolonged day action with his greatly superior opponent. The *Graf Spee* carried six 11-inch guns and eight 5.9's. The *Exeter* mounted six 8-inch, and the *Ajax* and *Achilles* eight 6-inch each. It was the Commodore's intention to close in after dark, and to finish off the business with guns and torpedoes.

It was soon clear that the *Graf Spee* was making for the River Plate, and the *Ajax* and *Achilles* continued to shadow. Just after sunset the *Graf Spee* fired three salvoes at the *Achilles*, to which the British cruiser replied. The German fired more rounds between 9.30 and 9.45 ; but they were merely intended to keep shadowers at a distance.

As the hammocks were still piled up in their room, the prisoners had turned in. The *Graf Spee* anchored off Montevideo shortly after midnight, and 10 minutes later an English-speaking officer came in and stood among the hammocks. " Gentlemen," he said, " For you the war is over. We are now in Montevideo harbour. Today you will be free."

" We couldn't believe it at first," one of the captains told me some months later. " You see we'd been asleep. Then we noticed that the engines had stopped. Someone hoisted himself up and looked through the broken skylight, and there, sure enough, were the harbour lights of Montevideo." There were cheers, and a babble of excited conversation. There was no more sleep that night so far as they were concerned. That same afternoon they were again free men. With them were Captain Stubbs and the four officers of the *Doric Star* already mentioned, including the Radio Officer, Mr. W. Comber.

It is known that the *Doric Star's* repeated wireless signals on sighting the *Graf Spee* on December 2nd were relayed from ship to ship and became known to Commodore Harwood, between two and three thousand miles away on the other side of the Atlantic on December 3rd. His three cruisers were scattered over two thousand miles, and concentration was vitally necessary if the raider, a pocket battleship, were to be met and brought to action with any hope of success.

As the Commodore, who by that time had been promoted to Rear-Admiral and awarded the K.C.B., wrote in his despatch of December 30th, 1939 (published as a Supplement to the London Gazette of June 17th, 1947) :

" The British ship *Doric Star* had reported being attacked by a pocket battleship in position 19° 15′ South, 5° 5′ East, during the afternoon of 2nd December, 1939, and a similar report had been sent by an unknown vessel* 170 miles south-west of that position at 05.00 G.M.T. on 3rd December.

" From this data I estimated that at a cruising speed of 15 knots the raider could reach the Rio de Janeiro focal area a.m. 12th December, the River Plate focal area p.m. 12th December or a.m. 13th December and the Falkland Islands area 14th December.

" I decided that the Plate, with its larger number of ships and its very valuable grain and meat trade, was the vital area to be defended. I therefore arranged to concentrate there my available forces in advance of the time at which it was anticipated the raider might start operations in that area."

The concentration of the *Ajax*, *Achilles* and *Exeter* was effected by 7.0 a.m. on December 12th. At 6.14 a.m. next morning smoke was sighted, and the *Exeter* was ordered to close and investigate it. Two minutes later she reported " I think it is a pocket battleship," and at 6.18 a.m. the enemy opened fire, one 11-inch turret at the *Exeter* and the other at the *Ajax*.

We know the rest, and the final outcome of the Battle of the River Plate. What one wonders is if that battle would ever have been fought if it had not been for those earlier wireless signals from the *Doric Star* and *Tairoa* a full 3,000 miles away to the eastward.

2

Among the 299 prisoners on board the *Altmark* were 12 other officers and 47 men from the *Doric Star*. The lot of these men was miserable indeed. Captain Dahl, of the *Altmark*, who had 12 seamen from the *Graf Spee* to assist in guarding the prisoners, had no love for the English. He had spent a considerable time in the First World War as a prisoner in England, and was now able to get some of his own back. He was a strict and unfeeling disciplinarian, and his captives were abominably fed, suffered through lack of exercise and water, and were crowded into makeshift accommodation, " furnished," if it could be called furnished, with bedding, carpets and miscellaneous fittings taken from captured ships.

As one who experienced it wrote :

" Number 1 hold of the *Altmark* comprised five compartments, each

*The *Tairoa*.

eight feet high, and originally fitted to carry stores or ammunition. The second one from the bottom was the room for the officers and engineers, the third one for petty officers and men. The room for captains, chief engineers and chief officers was a canvas walled one underneath the extended forecastle head on the port side, while a similar but slightly larger room was constructed for the Indians on the port side.

"The captains and other senior officers were later moved to the top 'tween deck space in Number 1 hold. The food was execrable—black bread, butter substitute, soup composed of fat, salt pork, with tinned and dehydrated vegetables. They had a small quantity of meat twice a week with rice or macaroni, and small slices of German sausage for supper varied by tins of 'synthetic' fish dyed bright red, or small blocks of jellied eels. The main hardships were lack of exercise in fresh air, which amounted to an hour-and-a-quarter a day, and lack of water."

As my informant says :
"There were no awnings or shelter on deck, and it was difficult to open one's eyes in the sun after the darkness of our prison with its perpetual electric light."

The water supply was precarious :
"We were given a metal bowl into which was poured our daily ration of one quart of tainted tank water, with which we had to wash ourselves and any clothes we had to wash."

Another prisoner says :
"We were in a compartment with iron hatches, forty-five of us altogether. It was a filthy place with no fresh air."

People involved in pettifogging breaches of the regulations were locked below for days at a time. William Curtis, of South Shields, one of the men from the *Doric Star*, testified that he was a prisoner in the *Altmark* for nearly 10 weeks. At one time :
"We were confined below for about a fortnight, without being on deck. They wouldn't let us see anything. There was very little food. We had black bread and tea, and didn't do any work. For a long time we got no cold water to drink. Sometimes we got washing water. The skipper, Captain Dahl, was a tyrant."

Until January 22nd, 1940, the *Altmark* was cruising in the South Atlantic, apparently waiting for orders from Germany. Then, homeward bound, she proceeded north, crossing the Equator on January 31st. On February 9th somewhere near the trade routes in the North Atlantic, she sighted various British vessels ; but managed to avoid them. The snowclad peaks of Iceland were in sight on February 11th, and three days later she entered Norwegian territorial waters, and embarked a Norwegian pilot, who took her south inside the three mile limit.

The attitude of the Norwegian Government was inexplicable. Twice the *Altmark* was stopped by Norwegian destroyers, and twice she was permitted to proceed. The second destroyer asked if the *Altmark* had any persons on board who were the nationals of a belligerent country, to which the reply was given that there were no such persons in the ship, which was a barefaced lie. The Norwegians knew, the whole world knew, that there were British prisoners on board. The only excuse the Norwegian Government may have had was that the *Altmark* flew the German state colours and was therefore regarded as a warship.

The Norwegian admiral at Bergen, however, was not satisfied, and on February 15th, when the *Altmark* entered the " Bergen Defended Area," she was intercepted by another Norwegian warship, whose captain asked to inspect her. This was refused by Captain Dahl, and the matter seems to have been dropped.

The prisoners were aware that the Norwegian coast was in sight, and had been keeping a lookout through a small peephole. They had instituted a system of one hour watches, so that nothing should pass unseen. Later on February 15th off Bergen itself, two Norwegian destroyers and two torpedo-boats approached the *Altmark*. One of their officers actually came on board to investigate. To be generous, his investigation was cursory to the extreme.

As Mr. G. A. King, Second Engineer of the *Doric Star* wrote :

" Another effort was made to get out, but we were repelled with hoses, and the lights were turned out. The officers made the attempt with the idea of getting the men out afterwards. All this time we had been blowing S.O.S. on whistles, and there were ships right alongside ; but we were still not rescued. The other Norwegian ships were within fifteen yards of us, and they could not have failed to hear the noise we were making. We broke the hatch with iron bars and banged on this until we were repelled. We had almost broken free, except for about a couple of inches, but when they turned out the light it was useless. They had turned on the winches to drown the noise, but there was a small scuttle hatch over the top of where we were, and we managed to lift this up. The Fourth Officer, Mr. Evans, put his head out of this hatch and blew on a whistle, and this was the time the Norwegians were on board. Two hundred and seventy-five men altogether made this racket, and it went on for fifteen to twenty minutes. We did not stop even when they turned on the water, so they stopped us by hitting us with pieces of wood and straps, and finally at the point of a gun. We knew that if we did manage to get out that one or two of us would probably be killed, but we were prepared to take that risk for the benefit of others. We were held up by the Norwegian destroyer for four hours, during which time we made a lot of noise. Then we stopped for five minutes, and then blew S.O.S., giving the international signal on pocket whistles. At six o'clock it was all over, the lights were turned on again and we were all terribly disappointed."

What orders the Norwegian Navy may have had we do not know ; but the *Altmark* was suffered to continue her voyage southward, escorted by a Norwegian torpedo-boat.

However, the British Government was aware that the *Altmark* was heading for home, and that she carried prisoners. And at about 2.0 p.m. next day she was sighted by reconnaissance aircraft of the Royal Air Force. They called the Royal Navy, and the *Arethusa* with the destroyers *Cossack* and *Intrepid* came in to intercept.

Though the full details of what happened have already been related, the story will bear repetition here. At about 4.30 p.m. the *Intrepid* closed the *Altmark* a little more than 200 yards from the rocky, ice-fringed shore. To prevent her coming alongside, Captain Dahl turned sharply to port and entered Jösing Fiord at seven minutes past five. It was covered with ice, though not thick enough to stop her.

The *Altmark*, which had Norwegian pilots on board, was still accompanied by the Norwegian torpedo-boat *Kjell*. The captain of the *Intrepid* at once asked the torpedo-boat's captain about the *Altmark's* British prisoners, to be told that the Norwegian pilots on board the German ship stated she had been examined at Bergen the day before, and had been authorized to travel south through territorial waters. The Norwegian officer also stated that the *Altmark* was unarmed, which was not strictly true as she carried guns either concealed or dismounted, and that he knew nothing of any prisoners, which was more peculiar still.

And so the *Altmark* entered Jösing Fiord, an inlet about $1\frac{1}{2}$ miles long with an entrance about 200 yards broad, but widening higher up to a maximum of 500 yards. There are many snags and hidden dangers in the approaches, and the entrance lies between steep, dark cliffs. The fiord, with its restricted anchorage, would not ordinarily be used except by small vessels with local knowledge.

Meanwhile wireless messages passed between British warships outside and the Admiralty, who were fully aware that the British prisoners were still on board the *Altmark*. Captain Philip Vian, of the *Cossack*, was instructed to propose to the captain of the Norwegian torpedo-boat that a joint Anglo-

Norwegian escort should accompany the *Altmark* back to Bergen for proper examination by the Norwegian authorities. This suggestion was declined by the Norwegian captain by order of his Government. Captain Vian then asked the Norwegians to accompany a British boarding party during the impending search of the *Altmark*. Again the answer was in the negative, so Captain Vian was under the obligation of acting alone. He did not hesitate.

The night was brilliantly moonlit, and at about 10.0 p.m. according to Captain Dahl's account, a warship passed the entrance and shone her searchlight down Jösing Fiord. Half-an-hour later she entered and stopped near the Norwegian torpedo-boat. The Germans took the new arrival for a Norwegian, their assumption being strengthened—according to Captain Dahl—by an International Code signal in morse, " Do you need a tug ? " and the reiterated demand, " Place a ladder at your stern."

Broadcasting some days later Dahl was injured innocence itself, quite oblivious to the fact that the *Altmark* had already illegally passed through some 400 miles of Norwegian territorial waters. " It appeared too extraordinary," he said naively, " that an English warship should enter a Norwegian fiord to undertake anything against a German ship." We again with morse lamp asked for the name of the ship, but received no reply. When the ship morsed " Turn about or I open fire on you," there could be no further doubt that it was an enemy ship which had thereby committed the greatest unthinkable breach of neutrality. I therefore commanded the crew . . . to swing out the boats, and sailed the *Altmark* further into the fiord, as a destroyer, which later turned out to be the *Cossack*, turned towards her. As in the circumstances it might be that the English would try to take the *Altmark* with them, I decided to strand the ship, or at least to damage the rudder and screws so that she should be useless. The English destroyer was thereby nearly forced on shore. As she passed, members of her crew who were standing ready sprang on board. They immediately spread over the whole ship. . . ."

By the most skilful handling Captain Vian had been able to lay the *Cossack's* bows alongside the *Altmark's* stern, and Lieutenant-Commander Bradwell T. Turner sprang across, caught a wire passed to him, and secured the two ships together. Turner was followed by a boarding party of two officers and

Mr. RONALD ARTHUR VESTEY
Born 1898
Senior Director of the Blue Star Line

30 seamen, the former armed with revolvers and the men with rifles and bayonets.

Rushing forward, Turner made his way to the bridge, where he found Captain Dahl and some of his officers working the engine-room telegraphs. They were stopped, but the *Altmark* already had so much sternway that she grounded stern first on the rocks, nearly taking the *Cossack* with her.

The rest of the boarding party, under a lieutenant and a gunner, were rounding up the German crew, some of whom had to be disarmed. Scuffles and scrimmages took place as the Germans were overpowered and put under guard, in the course of which Mr. John J. F. Smith, the gunner, was shot at and wounded in one of the alleyways. Meanwhile, a boat full of Germans had been hurriedly lowered and dropped on the ice, smashing it. These men remained in the icy water hanging on to the lifelines until rescued at considerable risk by the British. Some of the armed guard from the *Graf Spee* escaped across the ice with their rifles and opened fire from the shore. In the course of the whole incident six Germans were killed and others wounded, though on the British side no shooting took place until Mr. Smith was wounded.

Once the *Altmark's* officers were safely under guard, Turner took Dahl below to show him where the prisoners were incarcerated. The sentries with the keys had fled, so the bluejackets smashed the locks and burst open the hatches.

As one of the prisoner's relates :

"At about eleven o'clock we were keeping our regular watches when great activity was noticed on deck. I was on duty, and the next thing I heard was an Englishman shouting down to our hatch 'Are you British prisoners ? ' I answered ' Yes.' Then he said, ' You're safe. We've come to release you.' Then there was a loud burst of cheering."

So those 299 officers and men of the British Merchant Navy, including those of the *Doric Star*, came up one by one from the noisome places where some of them had been confined for four months. Mustering on the *Altmark's* forecastle they cheered and cheered again as Captain Vian turned the *Cossack* to bring her alongside bow to bow. Seldom can cheers have been more heartfelt than those which rang out in that moonlit Norwegian fiord on the night of February 16th, 1940. Landed at Leith on the afternoon of February 17th, the ex-prisoners found a great crowd waiting to welcome them, with the usual cohort of pressmen and photographers.

Thus Hitler's amiable intention of marching the prisoners through the streets of Berlin and other German cities in revenge for the defeat and blowing up of the *Admiral Graf Spee* and for the delectation of the populace, was frustrated. And while Captain Vian was being congratulated by the Admiralty for a feat which will go down to history, Captain Dahl was complaining bitterly of his treatment by the brutal English and their " violation of Norwegian territorial waters."

" The *Altmark* is now stranded," he reported. " Her rudder is broken, and one screw is damaged." Indeed, the *Altmark* remained aground for some time. Plucked off her rocky ledge by a Norwegian tug, she eventually reached Germany, remaining so far as possible in territorial waters, and limping all the way.

CHAPTER III

I

SULTAN STAR
February 14th, 1940

ON January 27th, 1940, the *Sultan Star*, a 16½-knot steamship of 12,300 tons, sailed from Buenos Ayres for the United Kingdom with 8,000 tons of frozen meat and 1,000 tons of butter. Commanded by Captain W. H. Bevan, she had a crew of 72 officers and men.

At about 6.0 a.m. on February 14th, when about 360 miles to the westward of the entrance to the English Channel, they sighted the cruiser *Exeter*, accompanied by what Captain Bevan thought was the battle-cruiser *Renown* and five destroyers, coming up from astern. The *Exeter*, indeed, was coming home from the Falkland Islands where she had effected temporary repairs after her severe damage in the action off the River Plate on December 13th. After exchanging signals with the *Sultan Star* the warship passed on ahead.

At about 4.30 p.m. the *Sultan Star* was suddenly torpedoed the starboard side aft, one man being killed by the explosion. An S.O.S. was at once sent off by wireless, and the ship started to settle. It was soon obvious she was doomed, so Captain Bevan gave orders to abandon ship.

The boats were manned and lowered, and before leaving the Captain went to the wireless office and spoke to Mr. P. Winsor, the First Wireless Officer, who was still tapping out the S.O.S.

" Come on ! " said the Captain, in so many words. " The ship's sinking fast ! You've no time to waste. You must get out of the ship with me at once ! "

" I can't, sir," said Winsor, still busy with his instruments. " At all costs I must stay until I get the All Clear."

And stay he did.

The *Sultan Star* was going down fast with a heavy list. The boat-deck was already under water, and the bows lifting in the

air.   Captain Bevan remained alongside in his boat until the
very last moment, and was nearly capsized and swamped as
the ship took her final plunge to the bottom.

Soon after her disappearance Winsor could be heard shouting
for help.   Wearing his lifebelt he was hanging on to some
wreckage, and after being in the water for about twenty minutes
was dragged into one of the boats more dead than alive.   But
his gallant persistence was amply rewarded, for within about
20 minutes of the *Sultan Star's* sinking, two of the destroyers
which had been escorting the *Exeter*, the *Vesper* and *Whitshed*
came back at full speed.   They located the U-boat, attacked
with depth charges, and destroyed her, afterwards picking up
all the survivors who were landed at Plymouth next day.

For his services on this occasion Captain Bevan was officially
commended.   Mr. Winsor was awarded the M.B.E. and
Lloyds War Medal for Bravery at Sea.   In his report the
Captain described how Winsor had refused to leave the ship,
even after orders to abandon her had been given, to make quite
sure that his messages got through.   Only then, with the ship
on the point of going under, did he jump overboard and take
his chance in the water.   To quote Captain Bevan's own words :

" I think this wireless operator, Mr. P. Winsor, is one of the bravest
men I have ever met since going to sea."

I have looked up the official London Gazette, No. 34857
of May 24th, 1940, in which the names of Captain William
Henry Bevan and Mr. Philip George Winsor appear.   The
citation fills in a few extra details, so I will quote it in full :

" On a fine clear afternoon the *Sultan Star* was torpedoed without
warning.   Her Master was on the bridge.   She at once began to settle.
The Master telegraphed ' Finished with engines,' the signal for those
below in the engine-room and stokehold to go to boat stations.   One
man had been killed, but the rest came up in good order.   At the same
time Radio Operator Winsor was tapping out the S.O.S.   The crew went
calmly to their boat stations where they were mustered by the Chief Officer
and reported ready.   The Master saw his ship was sinking by the stern
and at once gave the order to abandon ship, telling all the boats to get
well clear except one, which was to stand by to pick up the Radio Officer
and himself.   The boats got quickly away.   The Radio Officer continued
to broadcast the S.O.S. and the Master stood by him.   The ship's stern
was under water, and the water was over the after end of the boat deck.
His ship was going and it seemed certain death to stay another moment.
He dived over the side and struck out for the boat, which was standing by
for him.   As he was hauled into the boat he looked back for Winsor.
The ship by now was standing on her stern, her bows were in the air and
water was going down the funnel, when he saw Winsor leave the wireless

36

office and dash for the side. He was sliding down a rope when the ship went down. The next time he was seen he was clinging to some wreckage. The *Sultan Star* carried a deck cargo of some 200 tons in heavy barrels. These broke loose as she sank. No boat could have lived in the whirl-pool. There was, too, the danger of bursting boilers, so the Master waited for the maelstrom to die down, till it was safe to bring his boat to the rescue of Winsor. He could hear his groans as he was caught and pounded and crushed between the barrels. At last they lifted him on board, more dead than alive. It was not long before three destroyers arrived. They picked up the men from the *Sultan Star*'s boats, and sank the enemy. The doctor in one of them saved Winsor's life. Winsor's gallantry and devotion to duty had brought help to his shipmates and destruction to the enemy."

2

ADELAIDE STAR
April, 1940

At the outbreak of war the new 13,000 ton *Adelaide Star* was being completed for the Blue Star Line in Messrs. Burmeister and Wain's shipyard at Copenhagen. The contract for the building had been signed on February 22nd, 1938, and the ship was due for delivery in June or July, 1940. The vessel was launched on December 30th, 1939, and when the Germans occupied Denmark in April, 1940, all that was lacking to enable the ship to be completed in a few weeks were brass valves from Sweden.

After some correspondence between the German Embassy, the Danish Foreign Ministry and Messrs. Burmeister and Wain, in which the Ministry pointed out that the yard could not voluntarily hand over to the Germans a ship which was being built for British account, the Germans seized the foreign interests in the ship instead of the ship herself. The vessel was completed, the Germans having taken over the British contract, and was delivered on November 16th, 1940. All that is known of her fate is that in 1943 or 1944, after conversion into a raider or blockade runner, she was bombed and sunk off the Dutch coast by Allied aircraft.

3

WELLINGTON STAR
June 16th, 1940

The *Wellington Star*, of 13,000 tons and a speed of $16\frac{1}{2}$ knots. one of the finest ships of the Blue Star Line, was fitting out at Belfast when war broke out in September, 1939.

On May 12th, 1940, under the command of Captain Trevor Williams, she sailed from Melbourne for the United Kingdom with a general cargo consisting mainly of wool and refrigerated foodstuffs. Coming home through the " Roaring Forties " and round the Cape of Good Hope, she arrived safely at Las Palmas, Canary Islands, and sailed unescorted on June 13th. Three mornings later she was about 300 miles westward of Cape Finisterre, steaming to the northward at 16 knots and zigzagging as she went. The day was fine, with a fresh breeze from the northward, a slight sea, and full visibility.

At 11.2 a.m. the *Wellington Star* was suddenly torpedoed on the starboard side between Numbers 1 and 2 hatches, and started to sink by the head. Captain Williams gave orders to abandon ship, and four boats, containing the entire ship's company of 69 officers and men, were lowered and lay off.

A second torpedo was fired into the vessel, after which the U-boat came to the surface and shelled and set her on fire. The submarine then came among the boats and questioned the survivors as to the name of the ship and cargo carried ; but made no prisoners. She then disappeared, and at 4.45 p.m. the *Wellington Star* rolled over and sank.

I have no details of the subsequent boat voyages ; but three of the boats were picked up by a French ship and landed at Casablanca. Those in the fourth boat, which I believe was that in charge of Captain Williams himself, finally reached Oporto after a passage of eight days in which they suffered severe hardships. No lives were lost.

4
AVELONA STAR
June 30th, 1940

When war broke out the *Avelona Star*, a 14½-knot cargo ship of 11,000 tons built in 1927, was in port at Dakar, Senegal. Like all of the Blue Star ships she carried refrigerated cargoes, and towards the end of May, 1940, under the command of Captain George Ernest Hopper, she sailed from Buenos Ayres for London by way of Santos, Brazil, and Freetown, Sierra Leone, with a large cargo that included 8,800 tons of frozen meat.

The voyage across the Atlantic was uneventful, and reaching Freetown on June 15th, the *Avelona Star* sailed next day with the Commodore of a convoy which had gone on ahead. The convoy of 34 ships, spread over a broad front and zig-zagging with its escorts ahead and on either flank, was overhauled on June 18th. Twelve days later, at 10 a.m. on Sunday, June 30th, when the convoy was about 200 miles north-west of Cape Finisterre, one of the ships was suddenly torpedoed. An " emergency turn " was ordered, and the convoy continued to zig-zag, finally resuming its original mean course.

Several submarines must have been in the area, for about 12 hours later, at 9.30 p.m., the *Avelona Star* was torpedoed on the starboard side forward. As someone described it :

> " There was a dull thud and a huge column of water. The ship seemed to lift, and then settled with a twenty degree list to starboard. She righted herself, and then the foremost boiler blew up with clouds of smoke, ashes and steam which hid everything."

The *Avelona Star* was abandoned, and sank later. The survivors in their boats were picked up by S.S. *Beignon*, which steamed on and tried to overtake the convoy. At 3.0 a.m. the *Beignon* herself was torpedoed and had to be abandoned, sinking in about 10 minutes. Mr. G. L. Evans, the *Avelona Star's* Chief Officer, was asked if he would get some of his men onto a raft, which he did. His raft, greatly overladen with 25 people, was quite unstable and unseaworthy. Its men were sitting up to their waists in water, and it was lucky indeed the weather was fine. More of the *Avelona Star's* men were in the water, or in boats ; but there were not sufficient boats to accommodate everyone. The *Beignon* was a 5,000 ton motor-ship with a crew of only 30, and on board had been the 80 survivors of the *Avelona Star*. However, an S.O.S. had gone off by wireless, and at about 5.0 a.m. the destroyers *Vesper* and *Windsor* arrived on the scene and picked up 110 survivors from both ships, who were eventually landed at Plymouth.

Four of the *Avelona Star's* men were missing. They were probably killed when the torpedo exploded.

CHAPTER IV

I

ARANDORA STAR
July 2nd, 1940

BY reason of her exclusive pre-war employment as a cruising liner, the *Arandora Star* was probably one of the best-known ships in the world. Built by Messrs. Cammell Laird, Birkenhead, and completed in 1927 more or less as a sister to the *Almeda Star*, *Andalucia Star* and *Avila Star* for the fast passenger and refrigerated cargo service to South America, she soon became to be employed as a cruising liner for pleasure voyages to Norway, the Northern capitals, the Mediterranean and the West Indies. A twin-screw turbine ship of 15,300 tons with a speed of 16 knots, she was altered in 1934 and again in 1935, when her mainmast was removed. With her white hull and scarlet riband she sometimes went by the name of the " chocolate box " or " wedding cake."

When war broke out the *Arandora Star*, under the command of Captain E. W. Moulton, was on passage to New York, where she duly arrived. On her return to England she went to Falmouth where she was temporarily paid off. Visited by officers from the Admiralty and the Ministry of Transport to see what use could be made of her, it was considered she had too much top-hamper to be converted into an armed merchant cruiser. In the middle of December, 1939, however, the *Arandora Star* was sent round to Avonmouth to be fitted with the experimental Admiralty Net Defence and to undergo tests and trials to determine whether or not the gear could be used by all large merchant ships at sea and what would be the probable reduction in speed.

Throughout the war there were many suggestions for countering the U-boat menace, all of which were carefully scrutinized at the Admiralty. Among these proposals were various ideas for intercepting torpedoes, usually obstructions of one sort or another intended to be towed by ships on the flanks of the convoys. The only practical form of baffle was a light but strong wire net, something on the lines of the old-fashioned torpedo-nets used in the Royal Navy but not nearly so heavy, used by the ship herself. It was slung from booms, and rigged out whenever the state of the sea permitted.

It was this gear that was fitted in the *Arandora Star* at Avonmouth, after which the ship went to Portsmouth to have nets of various sized meshes fitted and tried out. The nets were made by hand in a large garage on shore by a gang of old seamen accustomed to wire splicing, and it was their boast that they could make a new set of nets of any given mesh in 36 hours.

At daylight each morning the *Arandora Star* put out into the Channel, ran her trials with the gear, and returned to the anchorage before dark. Any alterations to the gear were then put in hand for the next day's trials. " So far as our ship was concerned," one of the officers wrote, " the nets were quite easily brought up to a very fair standard of efficiency. With nets down, our speed was reduced from 15½ knots to 14¼. Turning at full speed, too, was successful, and during torpedo firing trials the nets trapped all of them."

Then, for some reason, though doubtless a good one, the Admiralty decided to abandon the experiments so far as the *Arandora Star* was concerned, and the ship was ordered to Devonport, to have the booms and other gear stripped.

While on the subject of these nets it may here be said that the Admiralty Net Defence was fitted to a few ships in August, 1941, while by the end of the war it had been provided for 700 vessels. It was never infallible, and covered no more than 60 to 75 per cent. of the ship's side. Of the 21 ships contacted by U-boat torpedoes with the nets streamed, six were sunk through the nets being penetrated or the torpedoes striking the ship in an uncovered part. On the 15 other occasions the torpedoes either exploded in the net, causing non-lethal damage, or else failed to pass through it. There was one case of a large ship filled with troops finding a live torpedo entangled in her nets when they were hauled up on arrival in harbour. Without being aware of it, she had been towing the deadly thing for 36 hours !

However, to revert to the *Arandora Star*. After the gear had been stripped out of her at Devonport the ship was ordered up to Liverpool for orders. There, lying at anchor off the Landing

Stage, she had her first experience of bombing, a solitary aircraft coming over at night and dropping a stick of bombs which fell between the *Arandora Star* and the battleship *Prince of Wales*, completing in Messrs. Cammell Laird's shipyard at Birkenhead.

Sailing next day, the *Arandora Star* found herself ordered to rendezvous with the aircraft-carrier *Glorious* and the anti-aircraft cruiser *Coventry* off Narvik, a place she must often have passed with her crowd of holiday passengers during happier summers on her voyages to the North Cape to see the midnight sun. On some date about June 4th she entered the fiord with other ships, and embarked about 1,600 officers and men of the Royal Air Force and some French and Polish troops. In all some 25,000 men were embarked from Norway in various ships, and were brought back to the United Kingdom under the escort of the battleship *Valiant* with cruisers and destroyers.

Until June 7th, at anyrate, the *Arandora Star* was in company with the *Glorious* and *Coventry*. The German battleships *Scharnhorst* and *Gneisenau*, with the heavy cruiser *Admiral Hipper* and two destroyers, were at sea. On June 8th, in the far north off Narvik, they sank the troopship *Orama*, the tanker *Oilpioneer* and their escorting trawler, H.M.S. *Juniper*. That same day, after a running fight, the enemy also sank the *Glorious* and her two escorting destroyers, the *Acasta* and *Ardent*.

The *Arandora Star* disembarked her troops at Glasgow, and then sailed for Swansea. From there she was ordered to Brest to bring out any troops or refugees she could. As one eye-witness writes :

" The bombers were very busy over the port when we got in, and were preventing anybody getting a chance to embark in any sort of craft. Only half-a-dozen got out to us, and we too had to clear out. A British destroyer came in to help us, and we got out into the Channel safely. She was being heavily bombed when we last saw her, and firing back with all her armament. She signalled to us to clear out with what survivors we had, and I hope they too got clear eventually."

The *Arandora Star* returned to Falmouth, disembarked her few refugees, and refuelled. Then she was ordered to Quiberon Bay, where it was fairly quiet and she took about 300 people on board, landing them again at Falmouth. She was next sent to Bayonne, where she was met by a destroyer :

" We slowed down," our officer writes, " but had to keep on the move as the bombers were busy again. This time there were dozens of over-loaded small craft adrift off the beach waiting for a ship to pick them up, so it was something of a job to get them all aboard a moving ship. However, we got about 500, if my memory is correct, and again crossed to Falmouth."

" The retreat down the French coast was becoming chaotic by this time," he continues, " and we were sent out to try and get down to the last port where there was any hope of getting survivors out. This was St. Jean de Luz. All was fairly quiet when we got in, and we got about 1,700 troops and refugees, including most of the Polish Staff and their troops who had been fighting back all the way down the coast. We got clear just as the bombers came over the hills, and strangely enough they left us alone this time ! We went to Liverpool with that load, and lay off the landing stage while they were disembarked."

It was there, on June 29th, after the most strenuous and eventful month of her career, that the senior officers of the *Arandora Star* heard they were to go alongside next day to embark a large number of German and Italian internees and some prisoners-of-war, with their military guard, for St. Johns, Newfoundland.

It was a prospect few people would have relished.

2

At about 4.0 a.m. on July 2nd the *Arandora Star* sailed from Liverpool. In all she carried 1,673 people, made up as follows : officers and crew, 174 ; military guard, 200 ; German interned males, 479 ; German prisoners of war, 86 ; Italian interned males, 734.

The weather was fine when the ship reached the open sea. Steaming at 15 knots and zig-zagging, she went unescorted. All went well until 6.15 a.m. on July 2nd, when the ship, steering west, was suddenly torpedoed in a position about 75 miles west of the Bloody Foreland, County Donegal. The Chief Officer, Mr. F. B. Brown, and the Third Officer, Mr. W. H. Tulip, were both on the bridge. Four extra look-outs were posted ; but no vestige of the submarine was seen.

The torpedo struck and exploded on the starboard side at the after engine-room, which flooded at once to sea level. Two engineer officers and all of the men below were either drowned or killed by blast. The turbines were completely wrecked. The main and emergency generators were put out of action, which flung the ship into complete darkness ; and all communications between the bridge, engine-room and wireless office were destroyed. One boat the starboard side was smashed by the explosion, and the davits and falls of another were damaged. The ship's position was being plotted on the chart

43

every half hour, and as soon as the torpedo struck Mr. Brown sent the position to the wireless room with orders to send out an S.O.S. It was duly transmitted and answered by Malin Head.

No sooner had the explosion occurred when most of the Germans and Italians rushed on deck and greatly hampered the crew in their work of lowering the boats. About 90 life-rafts were carried on the upper deck, and more than half of them were thrown over the side as soon as the ship lost her way. But for the time none of the foreigners could be persuaded to go overboard and take to the rafts. Losing their heads they rushed the boats, which had to be cleared before lowering with the help of the military guard. In the unfamiliar surroundings of a sinking ship these sorely-tried soldiers behaved magnificently.

However, out of a total of 12 boats 10 were lowered, only to be overcrowded by swarms of prisoners going down the side ladders and falls. The rest of the rafts were launched overboard ; but still many of the Italians refused to leave the ship. Many more lives could have been saved if they had behaved sensibly.

The list of the ship rapidly increased, and by 7.15 it was apparent she was about to sink. It was then that Captain Moulton and his senior officers walked over the side as the water came up to meet them. Even at this last moment many of the Italians could not be persuaded to save themselves by jumping overboard.

As Mr. Brown said :

" I was picked up by a boat after being in the water about twenty minutes. I saw nothing of the officers who left at the same time as I did. The vessel turned over and sank stern first almost immediately, and I think they must have been trapped as she came over."

And so, at 7.20 the *Arandora Star* rolled over, flung her bows vertically into the air, and went to the bottom, carrying many people with her. There were left on the heaving surface 10 lifeboats and an ever-widening patch of oil fuel littered with rafts, wreckage and the heads of swimmers. How many were drowned or suffocated in the thick oil one has no means of knowing.

Coastal Command of the Royal Air Force was quickly on the scene, for at 9.30 a Sunderland flyingboat appeared and dropped first-aid outfits, food and cigarettes in watertight bags together with a message that help was on its way. The aircraft remained circling overhead until 1.0 p.m., when the Canadian destroyer, H.M.C.S. *St. Laurent*, Commander H. G. De Wolf, arrived at full speed for the work of rescue.

It was a task of the greatest difficulty which took all of five hours. Picking up the people in the boats was easy enough ; but rescuing small parties or individual people clinging to rafts or wreckage required patience and great nicety of judgment, not to mention good seamanship. Few of the survivors could help themselves, or even grasp a rope, because of the scum of oil with which they and the sea were thickly covered. Sailors had to be put over the side with bowlines with which many of the swimmers were hoisted bodily on board.

A British destroyer, H.M.S. *Walker*, arrived later and scoured the area ; but no more survivors were found.

It was evening by the time the *St. Laurent* had rescued all she could find ; according to my count 868 people, who were safely landed next day at Greenock. With a thousand people on board, counting her own crew, the *St. Laurent* was a very crowded ship. How she cared for a crowd of exhausted survivors which completely filled the mess-decks, officers' quarters and one boiler-room, leaving a number to be accommodated behind the dubious shelter of canvas screens on the upper deck, is difficult to realize.

In this distressing disaster Captain E. W. Moulton and 12 other officers, together with 42 of the crew of the *Arandora Star* lost their lives. Of the military guard 37 were drowned, with 470 Italians and 243 Germans—a total death roll of 805 souls of the 1,673 carried.

CHAPTER V

I

AUCKLAND STAR
July 28th, 1940

THE *Auckland Star*, a sister ship to the *Wellington Star* had also been fitting out at Belfast when the war began.

Under the command of Captain David Rattray MacFarlane, she sailed from Townsville, Queensland, on May 25th, 1940. After calling at Sydney, Capetown and St. Vincent, Cape Verde, the fine, sunny morning of July 28th found her about 80 miles west of Dingle Bay, in the south-west of Ireland. There was a northerly breeze with a slight sea.

The ship had no escort, and was steaming at her full speed of about 16½ knots and zig-zagging, when, at about 4.0 a.m., she was suddenly torpedoed on the port side abreast of Number 5 and 6 holds. She started to settle at once, and at 4.30 the Captain was forced to give orders for the ship to be abandoned, telling the officers they were to stand by until she sank. Captain MacFarlane himself left the ship in the Second Officer's boat, and at 4.55 the submarine, which never appeared, fired a second torpedo which hit the *Auckland Star* in the engine-room and flung debris high into the air. The U-boat, apparently, was in a hurry to make an end of it, for at 5.15 she fired a third torpedo which exploded abreast of Number 2 hatch. About a quarter-of-an-hour later the *Auckland Star* rolled over to port, flung her bows into the air and sank by the stern, taking with her a large cargo, which included 10,700 tons of refrigerated meat.

The crew, in their four boats, set sail for the Irish coast. Luck with them, for on July 30th one boat reached Slyne Head lighthouse, County Galway, while the three others sailed to within 12 miles of Dingle, County Kerry, where on July 31st they met, and were towed ashore, by a fishing boat. Not a man had been lost.

NAPIER STAR
December 18th, 1940

On December 15th, 1940, the 10,000 ton steamship *Napier Star*, Captain William Walsh, sailed from Liverpool for New Zealand with a general cargo. She carried a crew of 82 officers and men and 17 passengers. As she was a 15-knot ship she sailed independently and was routed far to the north through a position about 300 miles to the southward of Iceland.

By December, 1940, the U-boats were starting to work further afield and were already hunting in groups. Germany was in occupation of the whole of the western coast of Europe from the North Cape to the frontier between France and Spain, which gave her many bases and made it much easier for the submarines to pass unmolested into the open Atlantic. We were woefully short of long range aircraft capable of hunting the U-boats in mid-ocean, while our available surface escorts were all too few for the work of accompanying the convoys through the danger zone.

By the end of 1940 we had already lost 37 destroyers, while many more were under repair after being damaged in Norway, at Dunkirk and elsewhere.

During the autumn we had received an invaluable contribution from the United States in the shape of 50 old destroyers completed during the First World War. But all of these ships had to be refitted and re-equipped with modern anti-submarine and anti-aircraft weapons before they could pull their full weight as convoy escorts. Moreover, as I know to my cost when voyaging in one of them from Halifax to the United Kingdom, they were not well adapted for use in the boisterous weather of the North-Western Approaches.

On the afternoon of December 18th, the *Napier Star* was some 300 miles to the southward of Iceland steaming to the westward at 13 knots. It was typical winter weather for the North Atlantic—blowing almost a full gale from the south-south-west with a heavy, breaking sea, drizzling rain, and the dark clouds racing from windward. The ship was plunging and straining, with occasional green seas breaking over her forecastle and sheets of heavy spray flying overall.

At 3.55 p.m. by which time, in Latitude 59° North, it was practically dark, the ship was torpedoed on the port side.

There was the usual shuddering crash and great column of water, which destroyed one of the lifeboats. The ship listed to port and began to settle by the stern, and the Captain had no alternative but to order her to be abandoned. Four boats seem to have been lowered, a task of extreme difficulty in the heavy sea with no lights at all beyond that of electric torches.

For an account of what happened we have to rely on the report of the Second Officer, Mr. John Wilson Thompson, who was the only officer survivor.

He left the ship with a boatload of 20 people including six passengers, three of whom were women. As he pulled away, the *Napier Star* was again torpedoed, and sank about 20 minutes later. He saw three other boats in the water, but in the fierce sea could not get near enough to hail them, so made up his mind to lie to a sea anchor during the night. Of his crew only four were seamen.

The wind rose to a full gale, and the great combers roaring down from windward became steeper and more and more threatening as the hours passed. The spray flew over them in blinding sheets. Seas breaking on board filled the boat to the thwarts, so that they had to bale for their lives. Everyone was drenched through and the bitter cold was numbing. Nearly everyone was seasick. Several times the wildly heaving boat was all but overwhelmed. Once, when the sea anchor carried away and they had to improvise another by lashing three oars together, she fell off into the trough and was nearly capsized. They used what blankets they had for covering the women ; but there were not enough to go round.

During that first awful night four people died of exposure, and when the wan daylight of December 19th came struggling through the tattered clouds to the eastward the survivors committed the bodies to the deep. They must have thought of their own chances of survival, which were slender indeed. The odds against any ship happening upon one small boat in that wilderness of heaving, breaking water were very heavy. Long before that happened they might all be dead from exposure.

All through that day, with the wind and sea as bad as ever, they rode to their improvised sea anchor. It was useless to think of sailing. Even if it had been possible the nearest land to leeward was the inhospitable, rock-fringed coast of Iceland, a full 300 miles distant. They might never live to make it, and that afternoon, as though to emphasize their situation, another man died of exposure and was dropped overboard while the Second Officer recited what parts of the Burial Service he could remember.

In those high northern latitudes in winter, daylight consists of a sort of subfusc twilight for two or three hours either side of noon. When the second night came before 4.0 p.m. they were all suffering from cold and exhaustion, some of them too spent even to eat or drink. Hope of salvation was dwindling fast, though wind and sea had started to moderate.

It was at about 8.30 a.m. next morning, December 20th, when the grey dawn had started to break, and the visibility was no more than three-quarters of a mile, that someone shouted that he saw the lights of a ship. They roused themselves from their lethargy ; but he was not believed until the boat lifted to the crest of the next wave and they all saw her.

With joy in their hearts they burnt flares and the ship altered course towards them. And presently, after what difficulties we do not know, the boat was pitching alongside the wall side of the Swedish steamer *Vaalaren*. Friendly faces were looking over the ship's side. They were lowering ladders. Someone threw a rope, which they managed to make fast.

Too spent and weak to climb, the survivors had to be hauled on board with ropes. Taken below, they were put between blankets and given hot food and drink. The friendly Swedes could not have been kinder. Three days later they were landed at Liverpool.

Those 15 people, which included all the three women, were the only survivors of the *Napier Star*.

In all, 84 had perished.

CHAPTER VI

I

AFRIC STAR
January 29th, 1941

DURING the First World War German raiders, disguised as merchant vessels, had been employed with considerable effect against our shipping. The *Moewe*, which ran the blockade twice, is believed to have sunk 50 ships in two cruises in the Atlantic, besides laying mines in the Pentland Firth which sank the battleship *King Edward VII*. But the 15 months cruise of the *Wolf*, during which she steamed 64,000 miles, and is credited with having destroyed 135,000 tons of shipping was more successful still. Apart from the vessels she sank in the Atlantic, Indian Ocean and Pacific, she laid minefields off the Cape of Good Hope, Ceylon, Australia, New Zealand and Singapore.

The *Wolf* was an 11-knot merchant ship of 6,000 tons, converted into a raider by providing her with a concealed armament of seven 5.9 inch guns, many smaller weapons, four torpedo-tubes, and 400 mines. In her long cruise she never entered a port until she returned to Germany with her empty mine compartments filled with prisoners. She caused a commercial and insurance panic when her presence became known in oceans considered to be immune to enemy action. In the First World War, as in the Second, U-boats in the Atlantic formed the spear-head of the attack upon Allied shipping. But surface raiders working all over the navigable globe created a diversion of the Allied naval effort and a consequent diminution of the offensive against the submarines in the all-important area nearer home.

It was hardly to be expected that Germany would not adopt the same procedure when war again broke out in September, 1939. The system of commerce raiding by well-armed vessels disguised as merchantmen had paid an ample dividend in the war of 1914-18. Moreover, in the course of 25 years, merchant ships likely to be used as raiders had become greatly more economical in their operation, and were able to keep the sea for much longer periods.

So it was no surprise to the Admiralty, but an added responsibility to their already colossal tasks of providing the ships for the defence of trade all over the world, when, from about February, 1940, onwards, German auxiliary cruisers, as the enemy called them, began to appear in the outer oceans where naval protection was necessarily sparse.

In this connection a recently published series of documents found in Germany after the war are of great interest. For the most part they were the result of notes taken for the Commander-in-Chief of the Navy during his conferences with the Fuehrer. Under the date January 26th, 1940, the Commander-in-Chief reports—" Five auxiliary cruisers are to be sent into the South Atlantic and Indian Ocean between the beginning of February and the middle of April. . . . Mines, among other things, are to be laid off Halifax and in the Persian Gulf." On May 21st, 1940, from the same source, we learn that one auxiliary cruiser was " detailed for mining off Cape Agulhas and for warfare against merchant shipping in the Indian Ocean " ; a second had sunk óne steamer in the North Atlantic and was " proceeding through the Pacific for minelaying duties off Australia and warfare against merchant shipping in the Indian Ocean " ; while a third was on her way to attack shipping in the North Atlantic.

By June 20th, 1940, five auxiliary cruisers were operating in the North or South Atlantic, the Indian Ocean or the South Pacific. On September 7th it was reported to Hitler that six mercantile raiders were at work all over the world, one " in the vicinity of the Behring Straits " ; that " operations, including replenishment of supplies at sea, have progressed surprisingly as planned " ; that success had " exceeded expectations " and that one ship had sunk 41,000 tons ; while—" there are strong indications of concern on the part of the enemy, who is not in a position to carry out extensive search activity." As a matter of interest, the raider reported as being near the Behring Straits had voyaged thither through the semi-frozen Arctic waters of the North-East Passage to the northward of Russia and Siberia, a truly adventurous undertaking.

In May, 1940, mines laid by a raider had made their costly appearance off Capetown, while in June another field made itself manifest off Auckland, New Zealand. In November more minefields were laid off Sydney and Melbourne, while the same month saw two merchant ships sunk by a surface raider south-east of New Zealand. Before Christmas another six ships were sent to the bottom on the long, lonely stretch between New Zealand and the Panama Canal. The loss of valuable tonnage was serious enough. But at a time when Britain was fighting single-handed against Germany and Italy and our naval defence was stretched virtually to breaking point, the necessary dispersion of our effort to cover the threat of raiders all over the world was more serious still. They were formidable vessels, heavily armed, sailing under false colours, and adopting every form of disguise. They changed their colour, shape, names and general appearance at frequent intervals.

One of these ships was the *Steirmark*, an 18-knot, 9,400 ton vessel built in 1938 for the Hamburg-America Line. Specially designed for use as a raider in the event of war, she sailed from Germany in December, 1940, after various alterations. She mounted six concealed 5.9 inch guns besides smaller weapons, with deck and submerged torpedo-tubes. She carried two aircraft and a complement of 400 officers and men. Known for some time as *Ship 41*, her naval name was *Kormoran*.

2

On January 15th, 1941, the 12,000 ton, 15-knot, turbine-driven Blue Star steamer *Afric Star*, built in 1926, sailed from Rio de Janeiro for England by way of St. Vincent, Cape Verde Islands. Commanded by Captain Clement Ralph Cooper, she carried a full cargo of meat, a crew of 72, two naval gunners and two women passengers.

On the morning of January 29th, after an uneventful voyage, when still some hundreds of miles short of her destination (Lat. 8°44′N. Long. 24°38′W.), they sighted a large ship flying the Russian ensign. For some hours the stranger remained at a distance, apparently keeping the *Afric Star* under observation. Then at about 2.0 p.m., the strange ship increased speed, approached the *Afric Star*, struck the Russian flag and hoisted the German, unmasked her guns and opened fire. Whether this was done before the *Afric Star* stopped and her crew had a chance to abandon ship I do not know ; but the British ship caught fire, and her crew took to the lifeboats.

The raider, which was the *Kormoran*, already described, picked up the occupants of the boats, sank the *Afric Star* by gunfire, and then proceeded on her way south.

Some days later the prisoners were transferred to the German supply tanker *Nordmark*, which was masquerading under the Stars and Stripes and the name of *Dixie*, and a few days afterwards to a ship called the *Portland*, a motor-vessel of 7,000 tons bound from Chile to Bordeaux, in German-occupied France. On the voyage a fire broke out on board, and the German guard, considering it was a case of mutiny and an attempt to destroy the ship, opened fire, killing one passenger and an able seaman of the *Afric Star*.

The *Portland*, with about 300 people from sunken vessels, finally arrived at Bordeaux on March 14th, the prisoners eventually being sent to internment camps in Germany. A deck boy of the *Afric Star* called King was repatriated to England. He had no idea of how it came about ; but having been called out of the camp he was told he was shifting quarters, and was sent to Naples. There he was put on board a ship of the Italian Red Cross which took him to Turkey, where he was transferred to a British hospital ship which landed him at Alexandria. After voyaging in several other ships he finally reached England via the Cape of Good Hope at the end of June, 1943.

The *Kormoran* met her fate at the hands of the Australian cruiser *Sydney* in the South Indian Ocean south of Java on November 19th, 1941, though the *Sydney* herself was sunk in the engagement, probably by a torpedo, In all, this particular raider sank nine Allied merchant vessels in the North and South Atlantic and Indian Oceans.

Though no further Blue Star vessels were to be sunk by German raiders, it is interesting to trace the careers of some of the others.

In a conference of the Commander-in-Chief, Navy, with the Fuehrer at the Berghof on May 22nd, 1941, mention had been made that four auxiliary cruisers were in operation, one in the South Atlantic and three in the Indian Ocean. *Ship 10* had returned to Hamburg after nearly 11 months absence during which she was said to have sunk 96,000 tons of shipping. Reference was also made to *Ship 33*, commanded by Captain Krueder, which was sunk on May 8th, by H.M.S. *Cornwall* in the western part of the Indian Ocean. Fifty-three survivors were reported on being taken prisoner out of a total complement of nearly 400.

"*Ship 33*," the conference report continues, "was the most successful German auxiliary cruiser, which carried out *extremely well* all the tactical and operational demands made of her. Her successes amounted to 120,000 British registered tons, including several prizes brought to home waters amounting to over 50,000 B.R.T. Three large whale ships from the Antarctic, carrying 22,000 tons of whale oil, were among the prizes ; also eight smaller whalers, a valuable tanker, and a steamer carrying wheat. At least two further ships, the names of which are unknown, were captured before the engagement with the *Cornwall*. Minelaying missions in Australian waters were brilliantly executed. Apart from sinkings directly caused by the mines (three to four steamers and one minesweeper have been sunk as far as is known at present), these mine operations have great operational effect with extremely far-reaching consequences for enemy shipping. The total success achieved by *Ship 33* exceeds that of the cruiser *Emden* or the auxiliary cruiser *Wolf* in the First World War.

"*Proposal.* These facts, together with the name of this outstanding commanding officer, should be mentioned and given recognition in one of the next reports of the Armed Forces High Command.

"The Fuehrer agrees."

3

An interesting sidelight on the mutiny among the prisoners-of-war in the *Portland* in March, 1941, came after the war, when the London Gazette of December 11th, 1945, announced the award of the British Empire Medal to Able Seaman Arthur Ernest Fry, of the *Afric Star*, and to Able Seamen Lynch and Merrett belonging to other ships. The citation ran :

"The S.S. *Portland* was captured by the Germans and, with a prize crew on board, was used to transport 327 prisoners to Bordeaux. A small group of prisoners led by Fry determined to regain control of the ship and bring her into a British port. Their plans were, however, frustrated. Subsequently an attempt was made to set the cargo on fire in the hope that the smoke would be seen by British naval craft. The enemy, however, succeeded in putting out the fire, though not until considerable damage had been done to the ship and cargo. Subsequently, at Hamburg the Germans sentenced Fry to death and his assistants to long terms of imprisonment on charges of mutiny and arson. The three men were subsequently repatriated and are now in this country.

"Fry was the chief ringleader and displayed courage and determination in pursuing the project of liberation by forceful measures.

"Lynch played a prominent part in planning and preparing for the attempted mutiny and fire.

"Merrett willingly participated in the execution of the plans and assisted Fry in the final preparations for starting the fire."

Fry, Lynch and Merrett, knowing they faced almost certain death, were very brave men.

CHAPTER VII

I

ALMEDA STAR
January 17th, 1941

THE *Almeda Star*, a 16-knot vessel of about 15,000 tons, built in 1926, was normally used for the passenger and refrigerated cargo service between the United Kingdom and South America. During 1939 and 1940 she continued on that service, sailing independently.

At 9.0 p.m. on December 22nd, 1940, while lying in the Mersey, she was damaged by a bomb during one of the air raids on Liverpool. The damage cannot have been very serious, for on January 15th, 1941, she sailed from Liverpool, commanded by Captain H. C. Howard, Commodore of the Blue Star Line, with a crew of 166 officers and men and 194 passengers.

The year 1941 opened with tempestuous weather in the North Atlantic, gale succeeding gale with dismal regularity. It spelt tribulation for all ships at sea.

The *Almeda Star* was unescorted. Suddenly, from out of the blue on January 17th, came her signal of distress. She had been torpedoed. Her position was 58°17′N. 13°40′W., which put her about 35 miles north of Rockall, that lonely hummock of rock some 225 miles to the west of the Outer Hebrides. No further message came through.

Destroyers and other vessels were at once ordered to search the area ; but without result. Not even a waterlogged boat was found, no wreckage, no trace of anything. Nothing recognisable as belonging to the *Almeda Star* was washed ashore.

Except that she sent off that one signal of distress giving her position and saying she had been torpedoed, nothing is known of what happened, even from German sources. We do not even know if the ship was abandoned, and the survivors tried to get away in the boats. All that we are aware is that she appears in the official list as having been torpedoed by a submarine in the position given. The weather at the time being very bad with a heavy sea, it is probable that the stricken ship was overwhelmed and sank in a depth of more than 200 fathoms carrying those 360 souls with her.

2

RODNEY STAR
May 16th, 1941

The *Rodney Star*, a steamship of 11,800 tons laden with the usual refrigerated cargo, sailed from Buenos Ayres on April 29th, 1941. Commanded by Captain Samuel John Clement Phillips, she was ordered to Santos, Brazil, and then on to St. Vincent, Cape Verde Islands, where she would join one of the escorted convoys homeward bound for the United Kingdom.

At this period of the war the U-boats were operating further and further afield, largely with the idea of dispersing our available escort forces. In April the first submarine had gone south of the Equator to try her luck on the route followed by our troop convoys to the Middle East round the Cape of Good Hope. A few more U-boats had been sent to probe for " soft spots " in the Sierra Leone area, where Freetown had assumed great importance as a convoy port through the closing of the Mediterranean to our shipping.

The United States was not yet in the war ; but the Germans were considerably perturbed by the " American Neutrality Zone " which had greatly hampered their operations within 300 miles of the coasts of North and South America. On April 20th Admiral Raeder was reporting to the Fuehrer :

" The operational freedom of our naval forces is considerably restricted, as, in some parts, the zone covers half the Atlantic. All contraband traffic from South, Central, and North America, moves as far as possible within the zone. The enemy can therefore concentrate his escort forces in the area where merchant shipping is forced to leave the zone, thereby making possible a considerable increase in escort forces and making attack difficult not only for submarines and auxiliary cruisers, but also for cruisers and battleships."

However, by dispersing his U-boat effort all over the eastern part of the North Atlantic, from the east coast of Greenland in the north to the Equator in the South, Admiral Doenitz stretched our slender escort forces to their limit. The main and vital supply line was still the convoy route between the United States, Canada and Britain. No escort forces could be withdrawn from there.

However, to revert to the *Rodney Star*, her voyage across the

South Atlantic was uneventful until the early morning of May 16th, when she was about 420 miles south-west of Freetown on her way north. The sea was calm; but the sky heavily overcast with occasional squalls of rain, when, at 5.50 a.m., she was torpedoed without warning on the starboard side abreast of Number 3 hold and listed heavily over to starboard. The engines stopped and two of the three lifeboats that side of the ship were wrecked by the explosion.

The ship was sinking, and at 6.2 Captain Phillips gave orders for the vessel to be abandoned. There was no fuss or bother, and within about ten minutes all the sound boats had been safely manned and lowered. They pulled clear of the ship.

The submarine had not been seen; but at 6.20 a second torpedo took the *Rodney Star* on the port side, and the ship flung herself over in that direction. The damaged boats, meanwhile, had been cut adrift, and the officers in charge of the others, realising they had a considerable voyage in prospect, went alongside them and helped themselves to their food, water and other stores.

At 6.50 a third torpedo exploded on the starboard side of the *Rodney Star* forward of the funnel. The ship broke her back, bow and stern lifting in the air and still afloat. At seven o'clock the U-boat surfaced and opened fire; hitting the bridge. She fired 78 rounds in all, which seems a waste of ammunition and effort, and several shells burst in the water near the boats. A little later a blinding rain squall came sweeping down from the westward, and the four boats took the chance, hoisted their sails and made off. They had orders to steer north-east and soon lost sight of each other.

Captain Phillips, and the others, made light of their boat voyages, though no doubt they suffered the usual hardships of overcrowding and discomfort. On the whole, however, the weather was good and no lives were lost.

After sailing for six days, the occupants of the Captain's boat were picked up by a destroyer and landed at Takoradi, on the Gold Coast. The boat in charge of the Chief Officer, Mr. J. Maclean, was under sail until 1.0 a.m. on May 24th, having made good 298 miles, when they were picked up by a French passenger steamer and landed at Dakar. The lifeboats commanded by the Second and Third Officers were picked up after two days and were also landed at Dakar.

Those landed at Dakar and thus coming into the hands of the

Vichy French were undoubtedly lucky in not being sent to a prison camp in the interior ; but in being exchanged for the crew of a French ship captured by us some time before.

3
THE *CANADIAN STAR* ESCAPES
July 19th, 1941

The *Canadian Star*, of 8,300 tons, was a new motor ship when war broke out. In July, 1941, commanded by Captain C. J. W. Jones, she sailed independently from Liverpool for Curaçao. At midnight on July 19th-20th, she was well out in the Atlantic about 650 miles west of Lands End zig-zagging on a mean south-westerly course for her destination.

The Chief Officer, Mr. P. H. Hunt, was keeping the middle watch. The lookouts had been relieved at midnight. It was a very dark night, with a gentle breeze and a slight sea and swell, and probably a good deal of phosphorescence in the water. Anyhow, half-an-hour later Mr. Hunt suddenly saw the luminous track of a torpedo coming in from abaft the port beam. Shouting for the helm to be put hard a' starboard, he rang down for full speed and summoned the ship's company to action stations. The torpedo missed. The U-boat was on the surface, and Hunt could see her. He steadied the ship to keep the enemy astern.

The U-boat fired a second torpedo which passed under the *Canadian Star's* stern, and then proceeded to chase. The big ship, meanwhile, was steaming at well over 16 knots, and realising she was escaping the U-boat opened fire with her gun. We are not told how many rounds were fired before the *Canadian Star* was hit in the funnel, which set it ablaze, a most unsatisfactory beacon during a night action.

It was very difficult to see ; but the *Canadian Star's* gunlayer at the weapon mounted right aft, William Charles Goody, was returning shot for shot, firing at the flash of the enemy's weapon. How long this continued the report does not tell us ; but the U-boat was quite close, apparently within a few hundred yards. The German's gun flashed, and the British gunlayer replied. Almost simultaneously there came another larger and redder flash from the U-boat which may have meant a hit. The result was not conclusive ; but the submarine gave up the chase and disappeared.

It was a very satisfactory action, for which Captain Charles James Whatley Jones and his officers and men received congratulations from the Admiralty. As the official letter said :

"The defensive equipment was used with such effect that damage may have been inflicted on the enemy. It is evident that the skilful handling of the ship and the spirited defensive action caused the enemy to break off the attack."

The *Canadian Star* was hit several times. It was later discovered that a shell entering on the port quarter had exploded in the after peak tank causing damage to the ship's structure. The shell that struck the funnel damaged the engine silencer, while a third shell bursting on the forecastle head damaged the superstructure, paravane gear and some of the deck cargo. Yet no member of the crew or any passenger was so much as scratched. There is no doubt that the *Canadian Star* and her people had lucky escapes, and would not have escaped at all but for the prompt and efficient action of those on her bridge when the attack took place.

Captain Jones paid a particular tribute to his Chief Officer, Mr. Percival Herbert Hunt, who first sighted the torpedo and the submarine, and at once took the necessary avoiding action, and Able Seaman W. C. Goody, the gunlayer. He also mentioned the gallant work of the Chief Engineer, Mr. Edgar G. Buckwell, and the Second Engineer, Mr. Bruce G. Sherratt, for trying to get into the funnel after it had been hit in an effort to find out and make good the damage and to put out the fire. The funnel at the time was full of exhaust fumes and gas.

For this most spirited and successful action it was announced in the London Gazette of January 6th, 1942, that Captain Charles John Whatley Jones ; Chief Officer Percival Herbert Hunt ; Chief Engineer Edgar George Buckwell ; and Second Engineer Bruce Graham Sherratt had been commended, while the gunlayer, William Charles Goody was awarded the British Empire Medal.

4

TACOMA STAR
February 1st, 1942

The 8,000 ton vessel *Tacoma Star* was a comparatively old ship, having been completed in 1921. She was commanded by Captain R. G. Whitehead. The vessel was in dock at

Liverpool when, at 10.40 p.m. on May 3rd, 1941, she was damaged by a heavy bomb during one of the air raids on the city. Set on fire she settled slowly by the stern on to the dock bottom ; but was subsequently raised and repaired.

On January 4th, 1942, she sailed independently from Montevideo for Hampton Roads and Halifax, where she was intended to join up with one of the convoys for the United Kingdom. By the time of her departure the United States was in the war, and the U-boats were already active in the Caribbean and the east coast of America. For the time being those areas were a paradise for the submarines. America had not had time thoroughly to organize her convoy system, and between January 12th and the end of that month the U-boats in the two areas mentioned destroyed 39 ships of nearly 250,000 gross tons.

On February 1st a distress signal was received from the *Tacoma Star* from a position about 380 miles east of Hampton Roads to say she had been torpedoed by a U-boat. Ships were sent to search for possible survivors ; but no traces of her, or of any lifeboats or wreckage, were ever found. It was the habit of the Germans to announce the successes of their submarines, and on February 6th an enemy broadcast stated the *Tacoma Star* had been sunk. Like the *Almeda Star* almost a year before, she unhappily disappeared with all her crew of 94 officers and men.

CHAPTER VIII

THE *EMPIRE STAR* AT SINGAPORE
February 12th, 1942

(*Note.*—The *Empire Star* was lost on October 23rd, 1942. See Chapter XI.)

TREACHEROUSLY, and without any declaration of war, aircraft from Japanese carriers bombed the United States' fleet in Pearl Harbour on December 7th, 1941.

America was automatically at war with Japan, and so within an hour, was Great Britain.

The Axis was finally tripartite—Germany, Italy, Japan.

The battleship *Prince of Wales* and the battle-cruiser *Repulse* arrived at Singapore on December 2nd. Seven days later air reconnaissance showed a large number of Japanese transports, covered by warships, in the Gulf of Siam. The two great ships sailed north to attack this concentration. They had no air cover, and on December 10th the *Prince of Wales* and *Repulse*, bombed and torpedoed by the enemy's shore-based aircraft, sank with the loss of 605 officers and men.

The Japanese drove south through the Malay peninsula, and the attack on the city of Singapore began on February 6th, 1942. In the early hours of February 12th the 10,800 ton, Blue Star motor vessel *Empire Star*, Captain Selwyn N. Capon, O.B.E., with the *Gorgon*, and under the escort of H.M. ships *Durban* and *Kedah*, sailed from Singapore for Batavia with evacuated naval, military and R.A.F. personnel, together with civilian refugees—men, women and children.

The *Empire Star*, which carried a considerable amount of R.A.F. equipment and stores, was a crowded ship. According to her Master, she carried more than 2,160 people, though as no accurate muster could be made this was probably an underestimate. Apart from 35 children, room had been found for more than 160 women, including civilian passengers and the nurses of the 10th and 13th Australian General Hospitals.

Air attacks were fully expected, and the presence of enemy

aircraft was first reported at 8.50 a.m. as the convoy was about to clear the Durian Strait, south of Singapore. The first attack on the *Empire Star* was made twenty minutes later, when six dive-bombers came hurtling down out of the blue.

The guns of all the ships burst into action. On board the *Empire Star* machine-guns and gunners of the R.A.F. were used to supplement the vessel's normal armament. One 'plane was brought splashing into the sea, to disappear in a sparkle of red flame and a pyre of curling black smoke. Another was hit ; to break off the action with smoke pouring from its tail. But nothing could stop the fanatical determination of the Japanese. The *Empire Star* sustained three direct hits, which killed 14 people and severely wounded 17 others, besides inflicting great damage and setting the ship on fire in three places. Two of the wounded were the Second Officer, Mr. James Duncan Golightly, who sustained severe injury to his left arm, and Able Seaman Charles P. Barber, wounded in the right thigh.

While the wounded were attended to by the medical officers of the R.A.F. and the Australian nurses, parties under the Chief Officer, Mr. Joseph Lindon Dawson, tackled the fires and succeeded in extinguishing them. It was a difficult and dangerous job in a ship thronged with people.

Intermittent attacks by enemy aircraft continued for the next four hours. They were high-level attacks from 7,000 to 10,000 feet carried out by twin-engined heavy bombers, as many as 57 being counted. A large number of bombs were dropped, some of which missed the *Empire Star* by no more than 10 or 20 feet. One lifeboat, which had already been damaged by blast during the first dive-bombing attack, was struck and completely demolished. The final attack was made by a formation of nine aircraft at 1.10 p.m., and once more the vessel, to use Captain Capon's own words—

" miraculously escaped with a series of extremely near misses on both sides."

Throughout these attacks Captain Capon took violent evasive action. In this respect he mentioned the " invaluable assistance " rendered by Captain George Wright of the Singapore Pilot Service who had remained in the ship after clearing the harbour, and the Third Officer, Mr. James Peter Smith,

" both of whom all through coolly kept the attacking aircraft under close observation, keeping me at the same time advised of their manœuvres and their probable and eventual angle of attack."

Captain Capon also stated in his report—

"Throughout this long and sustained attack the ship's company, one and all, behaved magnificently, each going about his allocated duty with a coolness and spirit of courage unquestionably deserving of the highest praise. It was fortunate that the damage caused by the three direct hits did not seriously damage the ship's fire service, and prompt action and yeoman service by the fire parties under the direction of the Chief Officer, Mr. J. L. Dawson, prevented any serious fire developing in the initial critical stage of the attack."

Writing from the *Empire Star* on May 29th, 1942, in reply to a communication from the Blue Star Line, Captain Capon observed that although the ship's company rose to the occasion —" in a manner and to an extent unquestionably deserving of the highest commendation," he did not consider that this justified or merited any special recognition, and that therefore he did not " advocate it."—" *Actually we*," he wrote,

"each one of us on board at the time, simply did our duty ; what, under circumstances of any such emergency, was commonly expected and required of us. In such circumstances, as I feel sure you will understand and appreciate, it is team work which so materially counts and that, in a great measure, accrues from example and leadership born of a high sense of duty."

In this particular instance, however, Captain Capon mentioned the names of the following as having given exceptional service—the Chief Officer, Mr. J. L. Dawson, and the Third Officer, Mr. J. P. Smith, whose gallant services have already been touched upon. He drew attention, too, to the work of the Senior Second Engineer, Mr. H. C. Weller,—

"whose co-operation throughout in the engine room and work afterwards done in the prompt execution of urgent temporary repairs was indeed exemplary,"

and the Chief Steward, Mr. C. E. Ribbons,

"who went to the greatest lengths in doing everything possible under the most trying and exacting conditions for both Service personnel and the civilian refugees then carried, and more especially in instilling amongst the latter that element of comforting assurance which means so much in eliminating in such circumstances any suggestion of or tendency towards panic."

Captain Capon's modest list of recommendations was considerably extended when it came to be considered by the authorities. He himself, having earned the O.B.E. in the First World War, became a Commander of the Most Excellent Order of the British Empire. The Chief Officer, Mr. Joseph Lindon Dawson, and the Chief Engineer, Mr. Richard Frederick Francis, were both awarded the O.B.E. ; and Messrs. James Duncan Golightly, the Second Officer ; Herbert Gordon

Charles Weller, Senior Second Engineer ; with James Peter Smith, Third Officer, the M.B.E. The British Empire Medal went to Messrs. W. Power, the Boatswain, and S. Milne, the Carpenter.

The following were officially " Commended "—J. J. Johnson, Junior Second Engineer ; J. Middleton, Senior Third Engineer; J. R. Mitchell, Junior Third Engineer ; C. E. Ribbons, Chief Steward ; T. S. Hughes, Second Steward ; R. Foulkner and R. Perry, Cadets ; C. P. Barber, Able Seaman ; H. E. Heaver, Donkeyman.

The London Gazette of September 15th, 1942, contained most of these awards, though because of the wartime, censorship and security regulations it did not mention the *Empire Star* by name. After describing how the ship left Singapore and was fiercely attacked it continued :

"The Master's coolness, leadership and skill were outstanding, and it was mainly due to his handling of the ship that the vessel reached safety. The Chief Officer showed great organising ability and tireless leadership throughout. Under the direction of the Chief Engineer, the Engineer Officers remained at their posts and kept the engine and fire service pumps working thus releasing all others of the engine-room staff to help the fire parties. The Second Officer was in charge of the guns and fought them with gallantry throughout the attacks. One aircraft was shot down and one certainly damaged by the combined fire of the ship and her escort. The Boatswain and Carpenter behaved magnificently throughout. They led the crew and worked tirelessly during the attacks. They were always present, leading fire parties, dealing efficiently with the fires and led parties that carried the wounded to hospital."

Such an official eulogy, which needs no embellishment from me, redounds greatly to the credit of the officers and men of the *Empire Star*, a ship of the Blue Star Line.

THE END OF THE " DORIC STAR "

This photograph was actually taken from the pocket battleship " Admiral Graf Spee " (two of whose guns can be seen in the foreground) just as the second torpedo reached its mark.   December 2nd, 1939.

CHAPTER IX

ATLANTIC BATTLE

I

SCOTTISH STAR
February 20th, 1942
AVILA STAR
July 5th, 1942

THE year 1942 was the worst year of the U-boat war, June, with 135 British and Allied merchant ships of 680,000 tons sunk, being the worst month. But our counter-measures, particularly in long range aircraft, were rapidly gaining in strength and efficiency. By the last week in August Germany had lost 105 U-boats since the beginning of the war with a total of 3,803 submarine officers and men killed, missing or captured. Indeed, as Admiral Doenitz, the chief of the U-boat arm pointed out to Hitler, this meant a loss of 38 per cent of the total operating personnel each year.

But more and more submarines were coming out of the German building yards, and in August there were 168 operational U-boats, about one quarter of which might be expected at sea at any one time. Most of the ace U-boat commanders of the earlier days were either killed or languishing in prison camps ; but there were still numbers of tried and trained men of seagoing experience who could be used to leaven the mass of new entries.

The stormy Atlantic was still the main battle ground, and at the end of September, Doenitz was reporting to Hitler that the increased number of U-boats in operation made it easier for them to locate our ships and convoys. Because of the shortage of Allied shipping, he said, our convoys usually travelled direct instead of by the more circuitous routes. The greatest menace to the U-boats, he added, were the increasing numbers of long-range aircraft.

2

On February 2nd, 1942, the *Scottish Star*, bound for Montevideo, sailed from Liverpool with a convoy. Ten days later, somewhere in the western Atlantic, the convoy dispersed. At 9.5 p.m. on the 19th, when the ship was about 700 miles east north east of Trinidad, she was suddenly torpedoed abreast of Number 3 hold on the starboard side. Hatches were blown off by the force of the explosion, and the hold flooded at once, the engine-room and stokehold also filling with water within ten minutes. The *Scottish Star* settled fast, so at 9.30 p.m. the Captain, Edgar Norton Rhodes, gave orders to abandon ship. In spite of the heavy swell all four boats were safely manned and lowered leaving the ship when the deck was awash. The captain, who was the last to leave, jumped overboard and swam to the nearest boat. Shortly afterwards, the U-boat came to the surface and fired five rounds at the sinking ship, then disappearing on the surface.

The boats lay to their sea anchors all through the night, and at daylight on February 20th two boats had drifted out of sight, leaving only one in company with the Captain's. He made sail for Trinidad ; but that afternoon three of the lifeboats were sighted and picked up by H.M.S. *Diomede*, which had intercepted the *Scottish Star's* S.O.S. The fourth boat, that in charge of the Chief Officer, M. C. Watson, reached Barbadoes on February 27th, after a voyage of nearly 600 miles as the seagull flies.

Four men of the *Scottish Star's* engine-room department lost their lives when the ship was torpedoed.

3

On June 12th, 1942, the Blue Star liner *Avila Star*, one of the Company's first-class passenger vessels on the South American run, sailed from Buenos Ayres homeward bound for the United Kingdom with a refrigerated cargo of 6,050 tons. Commanded by Captain John Fisher, she was a turbine-driven vessel of 14,400 tons with a speed of 16 knots. She carried 30 passengers, including 10 women, and a crew of 166.

Darkness on July 5th found her about 90 miles to the eastward of San Miguel, in the Azores, rolling gently as she zigzagged on her course and showing no lights. It was calm with considerable swell. Stars were shining overhead with a thin mist over the surface of the sea. Passengers and crew had been drilled daily at their boat stations. As the ship was passing through a submarine area all on board had been ordered to wear their life-jackets or to carry them, and always to remain dressed ready for any sudden emergency. Everyone had been issued with one of the small red electric lights run off a dry battery and designed to be clipped to the clothing. Intended to be switched on if people had to take to the water, they facilitated the work of rescue. Their use had saved many lives.

One of the best accounts of what happened came from the ship's surgeon, Doctor Maynard Crawford, who had previously served in the R.A.M.C.

After describing all his preparations in case the ship had to be abandoned, including the filling of a haversack with small amounts of brandy, sal volatile, iodine, dressings, a hypodermic syringe with morphia and other drugs, he went on to say that at about 9.5 p.m. he was sitting in his cabin typing out the medical report of the voyage, when there suddenly came :

" a tremendous rending crash and shock,"

which in some peculiar way reminded him of :

" the tearing up of thousands of frosted aluminium boxes."

Torpedoed on the starboard side in the boiler-room, the *Avila Star* lurched heavily over to starboard. The electric lights flickered and went out. The Klaxons sounded " Abandon ship," and crew and passengers hurried to their boat stations. There was no panic.

Number 5 lifeboat, on the starboard side, unfortunately came to grief while being lowered, her after fall taking charge and leaving her hung by the bows, spilling some of her occupants and most of her gear into the sea. Number 7, immediately abaft her, was lowered with her full complement of passengers and crew. In her was the Purser, Mr. Weston, and Doctor Maynard Crawford. As the latter described it :

" We descended rapidly and jerkily. . . . Next second we were afloat on the swell. . . . A sailor unhooked the great block most skilfully, and we had passed one danger. I tried to put in the tiller, but as I was afraid of its breaking until we got out a bit, I desisted. There was a shout of ' Mind the blocks !' The huge blocks by which the boat was lowered

67

were swinging to and fro like pendulums. Had they hit a head that would have meant a life."

Remembering his electric torch the doctor turned it on figures sliding down the falls as others shouted to them to jump or wait for the boat's movement.

"Things seemed going well. The Purser had his crowd off and we were floating easily. All this happened quicker than it takes to write it down. Except for No. 5 boat it was like a realistic boat drill."

At that moment there came another heavy shock, as a second torpedo struck and exploded immediately under the boat. It rose on the upheaval of water, flinging all the occupants into the air. The doctor felt himself fly upwards and then fall head first into the water. He rose to the surface, to find himself covered in thick oil. Wiping over his nose and mouth he was able to breathe. As he wrote :

"I heard nothing and saw no one. In some mysterious way I was a long way from No. 7 boat and the ship. It was horribly lonely. Then a fear of being sucked under with the ship seized me, and I swam straight out into the starlight as hard as I could. . . . There was a gentle oily swell, possibly due to escaping oil fuel, and I got well away until with great surprise I found myself nearly under the ship's bows."

Looking for a raft, he found himself on the port side of the ship, and getting very tired. Here and there on the grey swell he could see the little flickering red lights of other survivors in the water, and could hear voices calling. They were not close. Not knowing what to do, he lay back for a time and floated, looking up at the stars. He was not cold, and the least paddle kept the ripples away from his mouth. Then he found his left eye was half-closed, while his right foot began to get stiff and painful. He was hurt.

He had looked at the ship from time to time, and had noticed she was lower in the water. Her emergency dynamo had been got going, for there were lights on deck. But the *Avila Star* was sinking, her forecastle dipping towards the sea. . . . The water rose up to the base of the funnels.

The Doctor sank into a trough between two swells. When he rose to the next crest the ship had disappeared. About 200 yards away from the spot he heard, and felt, another rumbling shock soon after the *Avila Star* had foundered. It may have been caused by the explosion or shifting of the boilers, or by the collapse of bulkheads.

The time, approximately, was 10.10 p.m., one hour and five minutes after the first torpedo had exploded.

After some more swimming the Doctor sighted lights right ahead. Tired and aching he let go his precious haversack and divested himself of his outer clothing. Setting off on a slow breast-stroke, he stopped every now and then to rest and to use his whistle. His right foot " began to go queer " ; but finally, paddling on, he came close to a boat, so blew his whistle.

" Who's that ? " came the voice of the Chief Officer.

" Surgeon," was the reply.

" If you'll haul yourself aft by the safety lines we'll pull you in."

He did so, and laid hold of the gunwale with an oily hand. As he wrote—

" Several men hauled me in. How they gripped my oily clothes I don't know. And just when I was balanced on the edge my ribs and limbs seemed about to crack. I fell over on to the after thwart and lay there, the foot hurting quite a lot. But I was IN a boat. I had been something over an hour in the water."

Doctor Maynard Crawford was not a young man. He had a badly-broken right foot, a scraped left leg, one eye nearly closed, a cut lip, and three teeth missing. He was lucky indeed to get away with it, and to survive.

But much had happened since he had been blown into the sea over an hour before.

3

In all seven boats had been lowered, though as already described, Number 7 had been blown into the air and was useless, and Number 5 was leaking badly and had finally to be abandoned. Number 8, too, the motor boat, was full of water and had to be baled out before the engine could be run.

There was no doubt, as Mr. J. L. Anson, the Second Officer, wrote in his report,—

" that most of the casualties occurred at the time of the second explosion, the torpedo striking immediately under Number 7 boat, blowing its occupants into the air."

After all possible boats had left the ship, Mr. M. B. Tallack, the First Officer, found himself left on board the ship with Captain Fisher ; Mr. H. Massouda, Junior 4th Engineer ; and J. Campbell, a quartermaster. They tried to launch a raft ; but were unable to do so. Finally they found lifebuoys and oars and jumped overboard, Campbell losing his lifebuoy while doing so. Telling Tallack to join him in the water, the

Captain leapt over the side, followed by the First Officer.

"I drifted away from the ship," the latter wrote, "but was gradually pulled back alongside her, presumably by suction of the water rushing into her, and became tangled up with the paravane 'A' frame, from which I extricated myself, subsequently drifting away on the other side of the ship from which I had jumped. After watching the ship sink I tried to locate the others, and soon heard Massouda shouting for help, and Captain Fisher shouting for me. There was no sound from Campbell. I contacted Captain Fisher and we stayed together for about half-an-hour, supported by his oar and my buoy. Captain Fisher said several times that he could not hope to hold on long, as the cold water was cramping his stomach. He slowly lost his strength, eventually just letting go his hold and drifting away." Himself exhausted and nearly numb with cold, Tallack could do nothing to help.

"I drifted around for some time longer shouting for help whenever I saw a light from one of the boats," his report continued, "and was eventually picked up by Number 4 at about 02.00 G.M.T. 6th July. With the coming of daylight we made contact with the other boats and I transferred to Number 8 to take charge. I proceeded to pick up five people in the waterlogged remains of Number 7. Three of these men were badly injured. One was half paralysed with the shock, and another exhausted but uninjured. The man with shock, F. Walton, Printer of the *Avila Star*, died later in the day and his remains committed to the sea."

When full daylight came the boats gathered together and transferred and sorted out the crews as convenient. Number 5, which was making water badly, was abandoned. Mr. J. A. Gray, the Boatswain, was in charge of Number 1 ; and the Second Officer, Mr. J. L. Anson, in command of Number 2. He had with him the Third Officer, Mr. R. T. Clarke ; Mr. Brandie, Chief Refrigerating Engineer ; Messrs. Girdler, Ginn and Turner, Assistant Engineers ; five passengers, of whom two, Miss Traunter and Miss Ferguson, were ladies, and 28 members of the crew.

Lifeboat Number 4 was in charge of the Chief Officer, Mr. E. R. Pearce, while Number 6 had Mr. R. Reid, ex-chief Officer of the *Lyle Park*, who was being given a passage home. (His ship had been sunk by a raider in the South Atlantic on June 11th). Number 8 boat, the motor-boat, was commanded by the First Officer, Mr. Tallack.

Throughout December 6th the boats steered to the eastward under sail, though they were unable to keep very good contact because of their differing sailing capabilities. At about 6.30 p.m. Tallack started his engine and contacted boats Number 2 and 6, suggesting that as everyone was in a state of utter exhaustion it would be advisable to lie to a sea anchor during the night. Mr. Anson and Mr. Reid, however, preferred to remain on the move ; but asked that the three boats should try to remain in company. Tallack was unable to get touch with the other two boats before dark, and soon afterwards the breeze became very fitful. His boat was very bad under sail, and of course the supply of fuel for his motor had to be husbanded. He had 39 people on board, many of whom were smothered in oil fuel and sick as the result of it, while three were seriously hurt and another six at least had minor injuries, all requiring attention. Everyone on board was tired out, and in view of all these circumstances he undoubtedly did the right thing in deciding to drop his sails and lie to during the night.

At dawn next morning, July 7th, no other boats were in sight. Starting his engine, however, Tallack made contact with boats Number 1 (Mr. Gray) and Number 4 (Mr. Pearce) after running for about two hours. They kept sight of each other during the day, sailing slowly on to the eastward. They were still in sight of each other at daylight on the 8th ; but by this time Tallack was becoming seriously concerned about the condition of his wounded men. After a careful inventory of the water, provisions and fuel in consultation with Mr. H. Ellis, the senior engineer officer in the boat, and Mr. J. Hardy, Boatswain's Mate, who acted as his second-in-command, Tallack decided he would leave the other two boats and go ahead as best he could to make the coast of Portugal, nearly 600 miles to the eastward. Accordingly he remained under sail all day and at 8.30 p.m., just before dark, started his engine.

It was as well that he did so, for about an hour later lights were sighted on the port beam. Wild with excitement, Tallack at once altered course towards them, burning flares and flashing " S.O.S." with his torch. Lights could only mean that the oncoming ship was a neutral. Presently the boat was illuminated by a searchlight. The stranger was the Portuguese destroyer *Lima*, Captain Rodriguez, on passage from Lisbon to Ponta Delgada in the Azores. Tallack took his boat alongside and went on board, and was given the option of going to Ponta Delgada or not. Naturally he accepted, so his people were transferred, and the motor-boat sunk.

As he said in his report, the Portuguese captain asked if there were any other boats near :

" I suggested that if he steered west for about thirty miles he would most likely find two more boats. This he did, and Numbers 1 and 4 boats were found and their crews rescued, when I handed over my charge to Mr. E. R. Pearce, Chief Officer."

Two other boats were still missing, Number 2, Mr. Anson ; and Number 6, Mr. Reid of the *Lyle Park*. For them Captain Rodriguez searched for more than 24 hours, until, being short of fuel, he was compelled to continue on his voyage.

Mr. Tallack wrote :

"No mere words can express my feeling of deepest gratitude to the Captain, officers and crew of the *Lima* for their almost overwhelming kindness to us all. They did everything for us that lay in their power."

He mentioned also the following whose general co-operation was particularly helpful—Messrs. H. Ellis, R. Wilson, G. Bell, V. Rutherford and G. Hetherington, all of whom were engineers ; Mr. A. Sutherland, Carpenter ; Mr. J. Hardy, Boatswain's Mate, and Mr. J. Huint, Able Seaman.

He wished also to pay a tribute to the three seriously injured men—Captain Charles Low, of the *Lyle Park*, and Messrs. J. Owens and J. Alexander, of the Steward's department, who in spite of pain and great discomfort through their injuries never uttered a word of complaint.

Mr. Pearce, the Chief Officer, paid a special tribute to Miss Ferguson, a girl of 18 or 19, who had been in Number 7 boat when the torpedo exploded beneath it. Though covered with oil fuel and thoroughly wet, this brave young woman attended to and nursed four badly injured men in the waterlogged boat throughout the first night. The next morning, when told to transfer to another boat, she jumped overboard and swam to it. In spite of her condition, a report says that Miss Ferguson—

"was remarkably cheerful. Her behaviour and bearing were magnificent throughout."

4

We left the other two boats, Numbers 2 and 6, in charge, respectively, of Mr. Anson and Mr. Reid, on the evening of July 6th, when they were last seen by Mr. Tallack.

We have no details of Mr. Reid's crew, beyond the fact that his boat contained 23 people of whom two were passengers. Mr. Anson, however, was in difficulties from the start. At least half his crew were covered with oil fuel, while one had a smashed and bleeding left hand with a badly discoloured and swollen ankle ; another had sustained a bad cut across his left eyebrow, and a third seemed to have broken a rib. Some of the passengers, too, were in a bad way through dysentery and other injuries. They did all they could for the wounded ; but as Anson wrote :

> " lack of clothes and excessive covering of oil fuel over everything makes it hard to give any real aid to the two men who had the worst injuries and others suffering from oil and minor cuts."

The two boats kept touch with each other and sailed on to the eastward as best they could in a light breeze from the west-north-west and a calm sea. On July 8th, when they compared notes and examined the chart, they had sailed about 100 miles since leaving the ship, and had another 540 miles to travel before making the coast of Portugal. On July 9th Mr. Anson noted that the weather had changed to a fresh breeze with a moderate sea and swell, with clouds and rain squalls, while on the 10th the weather steadily deteriorated to a moderate gale with a long swell and a rough breaking sea.— " Craft making S.E. course," Mr. Anson wrote. " Pitching, rolling and shipping spray." That night both boats decided to ride out the bad weather and streamed their sea anchors, their occupants being made as comfortable as possible.

At 4.30 a.m. next day, July 11th, they hove in their sea anchors and proceeded under sail. The sea was still rough with a long swell, and the fresh breeze had veered to the north-north-east. At noon that day they estimated the Portuguese coast was 370 miles distant. At 8.0 p.m. that evening, in a very confused and uncomfortable sea, Anson decided it was prudent to use his sea anchor, so proceeded to stream it. Mr. Reid, in Number 6 boat, was unable to use his sea anchor, so the two craft parted company and never sighted each other again. To add to his anxieties one of Anson's injured men was worse, and during the night one of the male passengers : " showed signs of delirium and had to be carefully watched. He was rambling in his speech and wouldn't settle down."

Anson's boat was underway again at 4.15 next morning, making good about three knots in a fresh breeze and rough sea. They sailed on through the night, July 12th, 13th, with the male passenger still suffering from delirium. He was kept under control so far as possible ; but at 4.10 a.m. suddenly jumped overboard and said he was going for a bathe. Anson at once brought the boat into the wind, lowered his sails, shipped the oars and tried to reach him. For 50 minutes they rowed with all their strength against a rough sea and heavy swell ; but finally lost sight of him and had to give it up as hopeless.

The wind increased, and that evening, July 13th, Anson again streamed his sea anchor. " Most uncomfortable night," he noted, " Everyone wet through and miserable." They set sail again at 4.0 next morning, the weather still being very bad. The continued dampness and cold, combined with lack of sleep or any sort of rest, was not improving people's temper's. The man with the damaged foot had his injury rebandaged ; but gangrene was suspected. At noon, July 14th, Anson notes :

" Portugal appears to.be out of the question now owing to adverse N.N.E. wind and swell. Distance to Spanish coast 225 miles."

One of the crew was reported to have drunk sea water. They spent that night, the tenth after leaving the ship, riding to their sea anchor. They were rapidly losing strength, and by July 16th, one of the passengers suffering from dysentery was very weak, while others of the crew were unable to masticate their food. Seven ounces of water a day had been allowed since the bad weather had set in. The condition of the other invalids was unchanged, while the man who had drunk sea water was : " still not quite normal."

Food and water had been rigorously rationed from the start, and water was very scarce. The normal daily ration was 1½ ounces, or about one inch in the bottom of an ordinary tumbler, three times a day. This daily total of 4½ ounces was increased to seven ounces during the worst weather, though right at the end it had to be cut down to three ounces. At 8.0 a.m. each man was served out with one biscuit, with pemmican and two Horlick's tablets ; at 11.0 a.m. one chocolate ; at 12.30 p.m. two Horlick's tablets and two chocolates ; at 6.30 p.m. one biscuit and two Horlick's tablets. In all conscience it was little enough ; but, constantly wet with salt water, excruciating thirst was their principal torment.

They carried on under sail that night, July 16th—17th. The weather had moderated slightly, though there was still a breaking sea with heavy spray coming on board. It was bitterly cold after dark. At noon on the 17th they calculated they had 45 miles to go before reaching the coast, which was an underestimate. Indeed, it is probable that the speed of the boat under sail had been overestimated throughout.

It is unnecessary to continue the distressing story in all its detail ; but on the morning of July 20th, after lying to for the night, they found the sea anchor and cable had carried away. Mr. Anson had lost his pencil on July 17th, on which date his

74

log of the voyage ceased. However, another log was kept to the end by Mr. R. T. Clarke, the Third Officer.

The bad weather continued, and in the early hours of July 20th the passenger already mentioned died, and his remains were committed to the sea. On July 22nd, too, Mr. Clarke notes that another male passenger was found dead in the bottom of the boat, his death being due to natural causes and exposure. " Body committed to deep with those of members of crew who died from exposure and general weakness." More men succumbed before the final rescue.

To quote from Mr. Clarke's account of the voyage :

" *July 23rd.* 05.30. Robinson, A.B., at tiller reported that he thought he had seen navigation lights of an aircraft.

" 10.30. Two seaplanes with Portuguese markings circled boat and dropped three life-jackets attached to which were bottles, and tins of biscuits. Two were picked up.

" 11.45. Seaplane dropped a cylinder containing part of chart of West African coast and position of boat. Position given 34°00′N., 11°45′W. A message stated help would soon arrive.

" Noon. Distance run since noon yesterday 40 miles. Course E.S.E. (true). Gentle breeze. Slight sea and swell. Fine and clear.

" 18.30. Plane sighted overhead heading in N.E. direction. Probably Clipper from U.S.A. Fatalities continue among crew.

" *July 24th.* Deaths continue amongst crew. Bodies committed to deep and personal effects kept.

" Noon. Distance run from noon yesterday, 24 miles. Kelly improving but crew generally weak. Unable to masticate biscuits.

" 15.30. Aeroplane engine heard, but plane not sighted. Several members of crew over side swimming and hanging on to grab lines. Water seemed to do some good. Weather throughout light N.N.E. breeze, slight sea and swell. Cloudy and hazy.

" *July 25th.* Deaths continue amongst crew and bodies committed to deep.

" 10.00. Robinson, A.B., sighted mast of vessel. Flares burnt, also clothing, to attract attention.

" Noon. Crew picked up by Portuguese sloop *Pedro Nunes*. Sick placed in sick bay and remainder bedded down. Boat taken on board. One man died shortly after."

Thus, on the twentieth day after leaving the torpedoed *Avila Star*, 28 of her people were brought to safety after as terrible an ordeal as it is possible to imagine. One of the original 40 people in Mr. Anson's boat, Number 2, had been transferred to Mr. Reid's boat, Number 6, on July 8th. Ten people in Number 2 died during the voyage, another succumbed on board the *Pedro Nunes*, and two others in hospital after reaching Lisbon on July 26th.

The Portuguese officers and men were kindness itself, giving the castaways everything they wanted : " My greatest craving was drink, and I drank pint upon pint of tea, milk, water and coffee, and even that did not satisfy my thirst," wrote one of the survivors.

They had been rescued about 100 miles off the West African coast, and were lucky to be picked up at all, having, as one of them said :

"We hit the N.E. Trade Winds which drove us too far south and caused us to miss the coast of Portugal, and become becalmed off the West Coast of Africa. We were sailing without the assistance of instruments and charts, and had only our compass to steer by. This we checked by the sun by day and the Pole Star at night. We were unable to keep a true course.—The seas were so high for several days that I was continuously wet through. I did not get much sleep all the time we were in the boat. I just dozed sitting up, as until several died there was no room to stretch out.—It was hell in the boat, and believe me a still tongue kept a wise head. It was only faith in God, will-power to live to the last, and a strong constitution combined with tact that kept me alive. Several died because they lost all desire to live and would not help themselves. Some went insane."

Mr. Reid's boat, Number 6, was never heard of again. In all probability it was swamped or capsized in the heavy weather, and all its occupants perished.

Of the total of 199 persons on board the *Avila Star* at the time of the disaster 73 perished.

5

In the London Gazette of November 24th, 1942, it was announced that the O.B.E. had been awarded to Eric Reginald Pearce, Chief Officer ; Michael Bernard Millington Tallack, First Officer ; and John Leslie Anson, Second Officer. Miss Maria Elizabeth Ferguson, Passenger, and John Andrew Gray, Boatswain, were awarded the British Empire Medal.

The official citation for these awards is worth quoting :

" The ship was struck by torpedoes and sank in about an hour. The organization and discipline throughout were excellent. The Chief Officer displayed outstanding leadership both during the abandonment of the vessel and the boat journey which followed. He maintained steady discipline and kept everyone in good heart. The First Officer, who had been among the last on board, made a most creditable boat journey and brought many to safety. The Second Officer showed skilful seamanship while in charge of a boat which was twenty days in the open sea. He overcame many difficulties including overcrowding, sickness and damage to the boat itself.

" One of the passengers, Miss Ferguson, showed great courage. She sat in the stern of a water-logged boat throughout the night nursing four injured men. When the Second Officer's boat came up at daylight, she dived over the side and swam to it. She was covered with oil fuel but made no fuss about that and her general behaviour during the twenty days' ordeal that followed was magnificent.

" The Boatswain showed great skill and initiative in taking charge of a boat and was responsible for saving many lives."

In the same Gazette Captain Charles S. Low, a passenger, late of S.S. *Lyle Park*, and Mr. A. R. Sutherland, the *Avila Star's* Carpenter, were both officially commended.

In addition to his O.B.E. the Chief Officer, Mr. E. R. Pearce, was recognized by Lloyds by the award of the Corporation's War Medal for Bravery at Sea.

This does not end the list, for in the London Gazette of February 2nd, 1943, Mr. R. T. Clarke, the Third Officer, who was in the same boat as Mr. Anson, was also awarded the O.B.E. The citation is worth recording :

" After the ship had been torpedoed and sunk, one of the boats made a voyage of twenty days before being picked up. Great hardship was suffered through exposure and ten of the occupants of the boat died during the voyage. After seventeen days the physical condition of the officer in charge made it necessary to hand over control of the boat to the Third Officer, who throughout had been of great assistance. It was due to the courage, skill and fortitude of Mr. Clarke during the latter part of the voyage that the boat was brought to safety."

CHAPTER X

THE MALTA CONVOYS
1941-42

Melbourne Star, Sydney Star, Imperial Star,
Dunedin Star, Brisbane Star

In his despatch on the Malta Convoy of August, 1942, Vice-Admiral Sir Neville Syfret wrote of the Merchant Vessels :—
" The steadfast way in which these ships pressed on their way to Malta, through all attacks, answering every manœuvring order like a well-trained fleet unit, was a most inspiring sight. . . . The memory of their conduct will remain an inspiration to all who were privileged to sail with them."

I

MALTA, the largest and most important of the Maltese Islands, lies in the central channel connecting the eastern and western basins of the Mediterranean. It is 980 miles from Gibraltar and 940 from Port Said ; but no more than 60 miles from Sicily, the nearest point in Italian territory. Malta itself, with an area of 95 square miles, is about two-thirds the size of the Isle of Wight. Gozo, its neighbour, is smaller, with an area of 26 square miles. Comino, an islet of one square mile in the Channel between Malta and Gozo, is used as a quarantine station. Cominetto and Filfola are mere rocky islets.

With its population of about 275,000 Malta is the most densely populated area in Europe, and a greater proportionate number of people per square mile are able to support themselves by intensive agriculture than in any other part of the British Empire. With its fine natural harbour and dockyard, the island has always been the principal base of the Mediterranean Fleet, its commanding position making it of great importance for the protection of our trade in the Mediterranean. At the outbreak of war with Italy in June, 1940, it assumed a vital importance in the campaign, for it lay close to the lines of communication by sea whereby the Italian army in Cyrenaica had to be supplied and reinforced from the homeland. It became of immense consequence when the Italians in North Africa were later reinforced by the Germans.

When war broke out Malta was not adequately defended. Its anti-aircraft defences were weak and it possessed very few aircraft. Situated so close to Sicily, it was bombed from the day that war was declared. The devoted island probably suffered more air raids than any other portion of British territory of equal area. Our fleet had to be withdrawn to Alexandria, and in the early days Malta was no safe port for ships of any sort.

The wonder is that the island was never invaded, for the enemy had local command of the sea and, at one time, almost undisputed control in the air. For nearly three years, battered and virtually besieged, it had to be reinforced and supplied by sea with aircraft, guns, ammunition, high octane spirit, oil, food and a thousand and one other necessary items in the way of stores and equipment.

Here are a few figures. During the siege more than 700 aircraft were flown into the island from H.M. aircraft-carriers, and 111 from the United States aircraft-carrier *Wasp*. Up till the end of 1941 the large majority of the ships in the Malta convoys arrived safely, and in the first nine months of that year 24 ships discharged 146,000 tons of cargo. During 1942, the convoys became more and more dangerous. Between February and August of that year 85 merchantmen sailed for the island from Great Britain or Egypt, of which 24 were sunk and 11 had to return. Of the ships sailing from Great Britain 15 out of 40 were lost. Of the 296,000 tons of cargo shipped from Egypt 34 per cent. was lost. From Great Britain 314,690 tons was shipped and 43 per cent. lost. In all, 40 convoys sailed to Malta, eight of them from the United Kingdom.

Had Malta fallen, our situation in the Mediterranean would have been precarious indeed. It did not fall because of the supplies poured into the island by the men and the ships of the Merchant Navy guarded and protected by the Sister Service. To the supplies brought by the Merchant Navy must be added the precious aviation spirit, ammunition and food taken to the island by submarines from Alexandria, and the fast cruiser-minelayers *Welshman* and *Manxman* which ran the gauntlet alone.

The tale of the convoys to Malta from the west and from the

east has been told before. Time and time again, often with severe losses, they fought their way through to the beleaguered island, sometimes in the face of the Italian fleet, and always through intricate channels between the thickly-laid minefields in areas within easy striking distance of enemy shore-based aircraft. Clearer water was the hunting ground of submarines and " E " boats.

The story of those convoys is one of the most gallant of the war at sea—indeed, of the whole of our maritime history. But it cannot be told in full here. The account that follows describes the experience of some of the ships of the Blue Star Line—the *Melbourne Star* and *Sydney Star*, which were fought through from the west in July, 1941 ; a similar voyage in September, 1941, when the *Dunedin Star* got through to the island, and the *Imperial Star* had to be sunk after being severely damaged by enemy action ; and the most perilous passage of them all, in August, 1942, when the *Melbourne Star* and *Brisbane Star* reached Malta among the five surviving ships, mostly damaged, out of a large convoy of 14 vessels.

The latter convoy was the one of which Vice-Admiral Sir Neville Syfret wrote in his report the words quoted at the end of the introduction, and repeated at the beginning of this chapter.

2

The general plan for getting all the convoys through to Malta from the west was always roughly the same. From Gibraltar the merchant ships were escorted by one or more capital ships, an aircraft-carrier, anything up to five cruisers and about 18 destroyers to a position in the Skerki Channel north of Bizerta and roughly south-south-east of Cape Carbonara, the south-eastern point of Sardinia. There the capital ships and aircraft-carriers parted company and returned to Gibraltar with their destroyer screen, leaving the cruisers and rest of the destroyers to accompany the merchant ships on to Malta.

It is unnecessary to describe in any great detail the first convoy from the west in January, 1941, in which, to the southward of Pantellaria, the Malta contingent was joined from the east by Admiral Sir Andrew Cunningham, Commander-in-Chief, Mediterranean, with the battleships *Warspite* and *Valiant*, the aircraft-carrier *Illustrious* and nine destroyers. The force was savagely bombed, and the *Illustrious*, badly damaged, limped

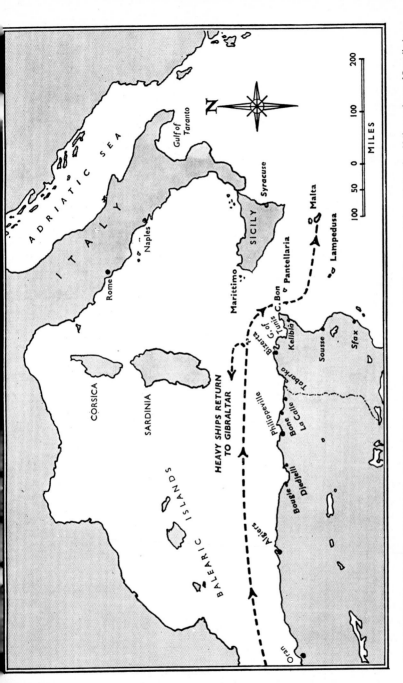

APPROXIMATE TRACK OF MALTA CONVOYS 1941-42

NOTE—Convoys of July and September 1941 passed east of Pantellaria.

into Malta, where she remained for 12 days subject to the fierce attention of the Luftwaffe. By this time some four or five hundred German bombers had arrived in Sicily and North Africa. From Malta the convoy of six merchant ships was escorted on to Alexandria, and during further heavy air attacks on January 11th the cruiser *Southampton* was sunk and the *Gloucester* damaged.

The Malta convoy from the west in July, 1941, consisted of six fast merchant ships, which included the 11,000 ton motor-vessels *Melbourne Star*, Captain D. R. MacFarlane, and *Sydney Star*, Captain T. S. Horn, both built in 1936. Captain Mac-Farlane was Commodore of the convoy.

Captain MacFarlane had already been in action. At the outbreak of war on September 3rd, 1939, he was in command of the *Imperial Star*, which had just finished loading at Melbourne. Armed with a 6-inch gun in the stern the ship sailed for home that afternoon. On some date in October, when approaching the British Isles, they sighted a U-boat on the surface examining a merchant ship. The submarine abandoned the search for a more profitable-looking target and made straight for the *Imperial Star* at full speed, opening fire as she did so. Captain MacFarlane promptly turned away at his full speed and opened fire at 3,000 yards. The second shell fell very close to the U-boat, whose captain, misliking this behaviour on the part of his intended victim, dived with great promptitude. The U-boat surfaced again later ; but the *Imperial Star* had the speed of her, and by adroit manœuvring was able to escape. The next morning, off the Scillies, they sighted a periscope ; but again were successful in evading attack.

The *Melbourne Star*, too, had had her tense moments when under the command of Captain G. Wilson. On October 5th, 1940, while on a voyage from Freetown to Glasgow and between 400 and 500 miles off the west coast of Ireland, the ship was attacked by a German aircraft. Several bombs were dropped and the *Melbourne Star* was hit by one which failed to explode. Dissatisfied with the result of this attack the aircraft then proceeded to rake the merchant ship's decks with cannon and machine-gun fire. One man, seriously wounded, died later ; but the ship escaped.

However, to revert to the Malta Convoy of July, 1941, the escort for the first part of the journey consisted of the battle-cruiser *Renown*, the battleship *Nelson*, the aircraft-carrier *Ark*

Royal, the cruisers *Edinburgh*, *Manchester*, *Arethusa* and *Hermione*, the cruiser minelayer *Manxman* and 17 destroyers, with Admiral Sir James Somerville in command. Trouble started south of Sardinia at 9.45 a.m. on July 23rd, when the convoy was fiercely attacked, the destroyer *Fearless* being sunk and the cruiser *Manchester* disabled. That evening further air attacks severely damaged the destroyer *Firedrake*. After dark the *Renown*, *Nelson*, *Ark Royal* and four destroyers turned back for Gibraltar, leaving Rear-Admiral Syfret with the merchant ships and the rest of the escort to fight their way on.

At 2.50 a.m. on July 24th the convoy was steaming southward in two columns about four miles to the eastward of Pantellaria, when it was suddenly attacked by " E " boats, which dashed down between the lines at high speed under heavy fire. Struck by a torpedo on the port side of No. 3 hold the *Sydney Star* listed to port, and for safety's sake Captain Horn decided to transfer his 460 troops to another ship. It was still dark, though luckily the weather was fine with a calm sea. The destroyer *Nestor* closed, and the trans-shipment of troops started in three life-boats. It was a slow process. The ship was still near the enemy coast with dawn approaching, so to hasten the business Captain Horn asked the *Nestor* to come alongside, which she did. All the troops were safely transferred by 4.5 a.m. ; but various members of the *Sydney Star's* crew transferred themselves also. The *Nestor* cast off and proceeded.

Meanwhile the holds had been sounded, and though there were 33 feet of water in No. 3, with something over six feet in No's. 1 and 2, the engine-room was dry with the machinery in good order. As Captain Horn stated in his report. " I therefore informed the Commander of the destroyer that I would make an attempt to reach our destination, some 130 miles off, under our own power." The *Sydney Star* was able to proceed, steering direct for Malta to save time and distance. She was leaking badly and the pumps were kept going con-tinuously. The *Nestor* was still in company, and with all the troops and some of his men gone Captain Horn busied himself in reorganizing his gun's crews in anticipation of air attacks at daylight.

The dawn broke fine and clear with a light haze over the horizon, and between 5.50 and 7.30 a.m. three attempted attacks by small groups of torpedo-bombers were successfully beaten off by gunfire from the *Sydney Star* and her escort. They had two hours respite, and then at 9.30 came more air attacks from high altitude. " Several bombs dropped in close proximity each side of vessel," Captain Horn wrote in his report. " Helm manœuvred to best advantage in evading bombs, and attack repulsed by ship's guns. One enemy 'plane hit and seen to lose height with black smoke pouring from his tail."

But the *Sydney Star* was too fat and tempting a target to be left alone, and at 10.35 she was subjected to another high altitude attack. Speed was increased, the flooded ship listing heavily as full helm was used for twisting and turning. Several bombs fell and exploded close to starboard, one particularly heavy one, which burst within 30 feet, sending its fragments over the fore-deck. It was a very near miss.

The ship was slowly sinking by the head. The water had gained in No's. 1, 2 and 3 holds, and was up to the 'tween decks. As the ship heeled over to the helm, so the water rushed over to the low side and held her there. Moreover, the list was gradually increasing. " By now," Captain Horn says, " we had arrived within 15 miles of our destination, so speed was reduced to 10 knots as a precaution against collapse of bulkheads, and later to 5 knots."

The *Sydney Star* entered the swept channel through the minefields off Malta at 1.45 p.m. and picked up her pilot off the breakwater about an hour later. Grappled by three tugs she was berthed safely alongside the dockyard by about 4.0 p.m. She still had a heavy list to starboard and was 12 feet down by the bows, drawing 42 feet forward and 29 feet aft. Divers reported that the hole caused by the torpedo was approximately 40 by 16 feet with extensive tearing ; but there was much other damage as well.

The main thing was that the crippled ship with her valuable cargo, was brought safely into Malta by the fine seamanship and determination of her captain, officers and men, and in particular the devotion to duty on the part of Mr. G. Haig, the Chief Engineer, and the people of his department. What with choked pumps and other damage, and the water gaining fast, the engineers had a most trying time. As Mr. Haig says, his engineers :

" Worked like Trojans, even though an aerial bomb exploded near the ship's side."

To quote Captain Horn again in his report to his Owners :

" You will, I know agree with me that we were extremely lucky to reach our destination, and will also appreciate the good work done by the crew who remained on board with me."

Repairs to the *Sydney Star* at Malta took nearly four months to complete. In this respect an official of the Blue Star Line who was flown out to Malta to superintend the work reported that :

" After many enquiries I am quite satisfied that the ship could not have remained afloat, even for a couple of hours longer. She would have sunk in deep water, but for the prompt action of the Captain in ignoring all routine instructions and making a bee line for Malta, taking all risks of minefields, etc., in doing so."

All the merchant ships of that convoy reached Malta with their valuable cargoes, and Captain MacFarlane and Horn were awarded the O.B.E. for their outstanding services. It is pleasant also to record that several more officers and men of the *Sydney Star* were decorated. Mr. G. Haig, the Chief Engineer, was awarded the O.B.E., and Mr. J. H. A. Mackie, the Chief Officer, the M.B.E., both of these officers also receiving Lloyds War Medal for Bravery at Sea. Mr. F. Bones, the carpenter, was rewarded with the British Empire Medal at the end of the war for " long and meritorious service with the Blue Star Line," while for their good work during the *Sydney Star's* eventful voyage to Malta in June, 1941, Naval Gunners I. A. B. Knight, I. W. Roberts and A. J. Robertson were all officially " commended."

3

The *Imperial Star*, Captain S. J. C. Phillips, and *Dunedin Star*, Captain Goronwy Owen, were among the nine merchant ships which sailed from Great Britain for Malta in September, 1941. The covering force, under the command of Admiral Sir James Somerville, was a formidable one, consisting of the battleships *Nelson*, *Rodney* and *Prince of Wales* ; the aircraft-carrier *Ark Royal* ; the cruisers *Kenya*, *Edinburgh*, *Sheffield*, *Euryalus* and *Hermione* with 18 destroyers. Of this force the five cruisers and nine destroyers under the command of Rear-Admiral Burrough in the *Kenya* were to form the escort for the last part of the run through the narrows to Malta.

At Gibraltar a good deal of subterfuge was used to mystify enemy spies who were known to be present in Algeciras and Tarifa reporting every ship that arrived or left. Escorting vessels requiring fuel arrived during darkness and sailed again before daylight. All the heavier ships leaving Gibraltar during daylight steered west, and only turned eastward after darkness had fallen.

The convoy and the whole of the escorting force passed through the Straits on the night of September 24th—25th, and later divided into two groups. One group, under Admiral Somerville, steered east along the African coast to give the impression that this was one of his normal cruises into the Mediterranean. The second group, under Vice-Admiral Curteis in the *Prince of Wales*, kept the convoy well to the northward on a course most likely to be clear of shipping and enemy air reconnaissance. In point of fact the first group was sighted by enemy 'planes north of Algeria on the morning of the 26th, while an aircraft with Spanish markings was seen by the second group the same afternoon. The two groups joined on the morning of the 27th, and were sighted and reported by enemy aircraft as they did so.

The first of the expected air attacks came between 1.0 and 2.0 p.m. when the convoy was south of Sardinia, the first wave consisting of 12 Italian torpedo-planes escorted by six fighters. The attackers were intercepted by eight Fulmars from the *Ark Royal* 10 miles from the convoy, one being shot down. Six, however, got through and dropped their torpedoes 5,000 yards from the convoy. Three ships had narrow escapes ; but avoiding action was taken and four of the enemy torpedo-carriers were shot down.

More torpedo-planes came in at 1.30 p.m. and though 14 Fulmars were in the air, three of the enemy pressed determinedly through the destroyer barrage and attacked the *Nelson*, hitting her with a torpedo on her port bow. Considerably damaged, the great ship could steam no more than 15 knots. Of the three attacking 'planes two were shot down by gunfire. Almost before this attack was over another 10 or 11 aircraft approached, flying very low. But the gunfire was too hot for them, and they dropped their torpedoes at long range. Two destroyers on the outer screen had narrow escapes, and one 'plane was shot down by gunfire and another by our fighters. Further attacks threatened during the afternoon ; but were intercepted by the *Ark Royal's* Fulmars. Of the 30 or more aircraft that had attacked, only 18 had come within firing range, to score one hit on the *Nelson*. Six of the attackers were shot down by gunfire, and four by fighters.

It was while these attacks were in progress that news came of the Italian fleet 70 miles away and approaching from the eastward. It consisted of battleships, cruisers and destroyers. This looked like an attempt to draw off Admiral Somerville's main force so that the convoy would be exposed to attack by light surface forces in the narrows after dark. As the *Nelson's* speed was reduced, Admiral Somerville detached the *Prince of Wales*, *Rodney*, two cruisers and two destroyers to deal with this new menace. Before long, however, news again came through from reconnaissance aircraft working from Malta that the Italians were retiring to the north, for what reason one does not know. Admiral Curteis's detachment was therefore recalled and rejoined the main body just before 7.0 p.m. It was now time for Admiral Somerville's force to retire to the westward, leaving the convoy to continue its passage escorted by Rear-Admiral Burrough's five cruisers and nine destroyers.

A few minutes after 8 o'clock Verey's lights were fired by a destroyer on the port wing of the screen as more torpedo-bombers came in to attack. This was avoided by a sharp turn to starboard. Further aircraft were in the vicinity about a quarter-of-an-hour later, and fire was opened as opportunity arose. The convoy swung back to the original course, and during these manoeuvres two of the merchant ships in the rear came into collision, though fortunately without much damage.

At about 8.30 the *Kenya's* radar picked up more aircraft on the port side at a range of about 2,800 yards, and closing. That ship and some of the destroyers fired a blind barrage, and a moment or two later a bouquet of sparks in the sky indicated that one of the enemy at least had probably been destroyed. At the same time the destroyer *Oribi*, stationed astern of the port wing of the convoy sighted an aircraft which was seen to drop a torpedo. She promptly opened fire with pom-poms and Oerlikons, and the 'plane, hit many times, suddenly burst into flames and crashed into the sea.

It was at 8.32 p.m. that the *Imperial Star*, which was in the port column, was struck on the port side aft by a torpedo, the explosion blowing away the rudder and both propellers and flooding the steering flat. The ship, though making water slowly aft, was otherwise undamaged. The destroyer *Heythorp* closed and took off 300 troops, leaving the *Oribi* to stand by the damaged ship.

The *Imperial Star* carried a very valuable cargo, so the *Oribi*, with what difficulty we do not know, took her in tow in an attempt to reach Malta. She towed for upwards of two hours, at times making good a speed of eight knots. The *Imperial Star*, however, minus her rudder and screws, was unmanageable. Moreover, the weight of ship and cargo was something like 20,000 tons, and at the best of times a destroyer is not the best type of ship for towing. At times the pair of them went round in circles, with the *Imperial Star* occasionally towing the *Oribi* stern first.

So at 1.20 next morning, September 28th, the *Oribi's* captain decided he could do no more. Slipping the tow, he went alongside the *Imperial Star* and took off the 141 people who remained on board. Three depth charges were lashed together just below the big ship's waterline, and at 3.51 a.m. they were fired. The explosion started a large fire, and the end was hastened by gunfire. An hour later, when the *Oribi* proceeded for Malta at 32 knots, the *Imperial Star* was ablaze from stem to stern and was listing heavily to starboard. As part of her cargo consisted of 1,000 tons of high explosive she blew up and sank later.

There were scenes of wild enthusiasm in Malta, with crowds of cheering people flocking the ramparts, when the cruisers steamed into the Grand Harbour at 11.0 a.m. on September 29th with guards paraded and bands playing. The ships of the convoy had a similar reception when they entered harbour about two hours later. The Maltese were fully aware of what they owed to the men and the ships of the two Sea Services.

For their services in the *Dunedin Star* during this voyage Captain Goronwy Owen and Mr. Harry Tomlinson, the Chief Engineer, were awarded the O.B.E., while the Chief Officer, Mr. Frederick Newman Johnson, received the M.B.E. These honours appeared in the London Gazette of February 3rd, 1942, with the following citation :

" The ship was attacked by torpedo-bombers but succeeded in drawing them off. Later she was machine-gunned by enemy aircraft, and then attacked by torpedo-bombers. By the skilful seamanship of the Master she avoided damage. The Chief Engineer answered with efficiency the many heavy calls made on his department. The Chief Officer organized the defences of the ship and more than one bomber was hit."

This was the last of the Gibraltar-Malta convoys during 1941, 29 merchant ships having been fought through to Malta with the loss of one sunk and two damaged. The casualties among the escorting ships had been a good deal heavier.

From the point of view of the war at sea our prospects for
1942 were far from favourable. The Japanese had bombed
the United States' fleet in Pearl Harbour on December 7th,
1941, so America was in the struggle as our ally. At the same
time, as Japan was now an enemy, our naval and maritime
commitments in the Pacific and Indian Oceans were greatly
increased.

The U-boat war still raged in the Atlantic ; but though it
was encouraging to know that our anti-submarine measures
were gradually gaining ground, optimism was premature. In
September, 1941, no fewer than 53 British, Allied and Neutral
merchant ships of more than 200,000 tons had been sunk by
U-boats, one slow convoy homeward bound losing a quarter
of its 64 ships in a series of attacks lasting four days. The last
three months of 1941 was a period of exceptionally bad weather
in the North Atlantic. It reacted against the activity of the
submarines, so that losses fell to 32 ships in October, 12 in
November, and 25 in December. However, the heavy gales
which followed each other in rapid succession spelt tribulation
for the convoy escorts no less than for the merchant ships.
Entire convoys were scattered or forced to heave to, while many
ships had to put back through storm damage or mechanical
breakdowns. With a large number of ships in ballast and
therefore difficult to handle in a seaway, straggling increased,
which added greatly to the cares and anxieties of the escort
commanders and convoy commodores.

The entry of America into the war in December, 1941,
provided the German U-boat command with new and welcome
theatres of operation. No fewer than 260 U-boats were now
available, and towards the end of the year about 20 U-boats
sailed for their new hunting ground off the east coast of the
United States. The first sinkings took place on January 12th,
1942. American shipping usually sailed unescorted, and avoiding the few escorted convoys the submarines concentrated
all the venom of their attacks upon such focal areas as Hampton
Roads, North Carolina and Cape Hatteras. The east coast
of the United States, became, as a German prisoner said, " the
U-boats paradise." Before the end of January they had
destroyed 39 ships of nearly 250,000 tons, of which 18 were
tankers.

In February, the larger U-boats were sent into the Caribbean to attack the oil traffic at its source, in the Gulf of Venezuela, and off Aruba and Curaçao. The anti-submarine forces in those areas were weak, and in the course of the month another 22 tankers were sunk in the Caribbean. In January and February combined, in all areas, U-boats accounted for 144 ships of nearly 800,000 tons, while further east near the British Isles German aircraft destroyed another 44 vessels of about 200,000 tons. The offensive in the Caribbean slackened during March, no doubt because operations there could only be carried out by the larger U-boats of which the enemy had comparatively few. But off the American coast the smaller boats still had good hunting, and in March the losses through U-boat action reached a new peak figure of more than 500,000 tons, 94 ships, of which a substantial number were tankers.

There was an excellent reason for a concentrated German attack upon shipping in American waters. Except for the convoys which had to be fought through to beleaguered Malta with heavy loss, the Mediterranean was virtually closed to our shipping. With Japan in the war and in possession of the sources of oil in Borneo and the Dutch East Indies, and with Japanese surface raiders and submarines at large in the Indian Ocean threatening the oil supplies from the Persian Gulf, the provision of fuel to Britain from the east in long voyages round the Cape of Good Hope was precarious in the extreme, and in any case totally insufficient for our needs. We had to rely upon oil from the west, from Aruba, Curaçao, and the Gulf of Venezuela and Mexico. A stream of tankers passed out of the Caribbean and Gulf of Mexico and up the east coast of the United States before voyaging across the Atlantic in convoy. To Britain fuel meant everything—fuel for ships, petrol for aeroplanes and a mechanised army, and oil for a hundred and one different industrial and commercial uses. The Germans fully realised that if this vital pipe-line were cut at or near its source, Britain would be forced to sue for peace before the American war effort gathered impetus.

In the Mediterranean, too, the war at sea had become more and more a battle for supplies, in which Malta was of vital importance. Submarines and aircraft based on the island, with cruisers, destroyers and submarines from the Eastern Mediterranean, were taking a heavy toll on the shipping which supplied Rommel's army in Cyrenaica. To the Germans it was manifest that if these depredations on the supply line to the Afrika Korps could not be stopped, Rommel would be faced with defeat at the hands of the British Army from Egypt. His only hope of removing the threat to his vital supply line was to increase the scale of attack upon Malta. So early in 1942 the bombing of that devoted island became redoubled in its fury. Most of the airfields were knocked out, while the Malta submarines often spent much of their daylight harbour time under water. With the anti-aircraft guns perpetually in action, the supply of ammunition to the island became an urgent necessity.

It is unnecessary here to describe the convoys from the east and from the west that sailed for Malta in January, February, March and June, 1942. Not all were successful. By August, however, Rommel's army in North Africa was already in difficulties. All the same, supplies to Malta were still of prime importance. Spitfires flown in to the island had wrought havoc with the enemy bombers, with the result that the continued bombing had ceased. But the Spitfires still required fuel ; the guns, ammunition ; the dockyard, materials for repair of ships ; and the teeming inhabitants, food.

The Luftwaffe, greatly reinforced, had lost none of its potency, and convoys had still to be fought through. So the convoy of 14 merchant ships, which left England in August for Malta under the command of Vice-Admiral Sir Neville Syfret had an unusually powerful escort. It consisted of the battleships *Nelson* and *Rodney*, the aircraft-carriers *Indomitable*, *Victorious*, *Eagle* and *Furious*, seven cruisers and 25 destroyers. Rear-Admiral Burrough was in charge of the ships going on to Malta. Among the merchant ships were the *Melbourne Star*, Captain David R. MacFarlane, O.B.E., and the *Brisbane Star*, Captain F. N. Riley.

Captain MacFarlane's ship carried all the ingredients for creating a minor earthquake. Her cargo consisted of 1,350 tons of high octane spirit, 700 tons of kerosene, 1,450 tons of high explosive shell and cartridges, with several thousand tons of heavy oil. The large convoy was shadowed by enemy aircraft for several days before entering the Mediterranean. Gibraltar was passed at 2.0 a.m. on August 9th in a dense fog which cleared by daylight.

On the 11th, at about 1.0 p.m., the *Eagle* was sunk 80 miles north of Algiers by a salvo of torpedoes from a U-boat. Captain MacFarlane saw her heeling over badly. As he wrote :

" The 'planes were slipping off her decks into the sea. I also saw what appeared to me to be an attempt by a pilot to take his 'plane off. He managed to turn it round, but owing to the heeling of the ship he was unable to do so, which was perhaps just as well. If he had succeeded, I think he would have swept many men into the sea."

Heavy bombing attacks started late that afternoon and continued until after dark. "After darkness had set in," MacFarlane wrote, " I saw several of what appeared to be our own 'planes returning from chasing the enemy. They couldn't alight on the carriers, so the pilots had to bale out and be picked up by destroyers, allowing their aircraft to crash."

The night was quiet ; but at daylight next morning, August 12th, bombing attacks began and continued with increasing fury throughout the day. At about noon, not far from Galita Island, off the coast of Tunisia, the Blue Funnel liner *Deucalion* sustained one direct hit and five near misses. Left behind, she struggled on at her best speed of 10 knots ; but at 9.20 p.m. was hit by a torpedo dropped by one of two torpedo-bombers coming in low. "The starboard tail shaft snapped," her captain reported. " The octane spirit ignited immediately, and flames rose to twice the height of the mast. In a few minutes the stern part of the ship was a blazing inferno, and I realized she was doomed." Her gallant men could do no more. Boats were lowered, and the survivors abandoned ship. She was still burning fiercely, with the after deck awash and ammunition exploding at intervals. She sank soon afterwards.

Meanwhile much had happened. The reliable Captain MacFarlane, of the *Melbourne Star*, must tell the story. He saw all that happened. " At about 7.0 p.m., just before the battleships and aircraft-carriers, with their cruisers and destroyer escorts were due to leave us, a very heavy air attack developed. The dive-bombers concentrated on the *Indomitable*, scoring direct hits on her flight decks fore and aft, causing fires. It was a most impressive sight to see her guns blazing furiously out through the smoke and flame, and later to see her steaming westward towards the setting sun, with her fires still burning fiercely."

At about 9.0 p.m., when the convoy for Malta was changing its formation from four columns into two, it was furiously attacked by submarines, torpedo-bombers, high-level bombers and dive-bombers. The cruiser *Nigeria* was torpedoed and damaged. The *Empire Hope* was bombed and set on fire, and

91

later had to be sunk by one of the escorts, towing being impossible. The *Clan Ferguson* was torpedoed and blew up, and the tanker *Ohio* torpedoed by a submarine and then heavily bombed. Eyewitnesses, seeing the explosions and the ship on fire, thought she had gone. But continuously attacked by aircraft she struggled on to Malta, arriving three days later with much of her valuable cargo intact. Her battered remains were not worth salving.

The anti-aircraft cruiser *Cairo*, torpedoed by a U-boat, had to be sunk as towing was impossible. The *Brisbane Star* was torpedoed and had her bows blown away. The gallant Captain Riley refused to abandon her saying—" If we don't go down with the ship, we'll go to Malta. We *are* going to Malta." She could only steam three knots, and was in a sinking condition. She eventually reached Malta ; but of her adventures I shall write later.

The *Melbourne Star* had been in the thick of it. Just after the *Ohio* was torpedoed, she had to alter course abruptly to avoid collision. Separated from the main convoy, in which several of the ships were blazing with towering piles of black smoke wreathing to the sky, MacFarlane could see no escorts anywhere near. They were otherwise engaged. Passing close to an American ship, the *Santa Elisa*, he hailed her by megaphone. " I'm going on to Malta ! " he shouted. " Will you follow ? "

The answer came " Yes ! " and the *Santa Elisa* fell in astern. MacFarlane thought that another ship followed the American.

The *Melbourne Star* increased to full speed. It was dark, with the light on Cape Bon winking clear on the starboard bow. A destroyer came up from astern. " Shall I follow you ? " MacFarlane asked, to which the destroyer replied " Yes. Follow me," which he did. They rounded Cape Bon and proceeded to the southward inside the minefields until they came upon a disabled cruiser. " The destroyer hauled in towards her," MacFarlane wrote. " We followed ; but she signalled to us to carry on, which we did. A short time later the destroyer reappeared out of the darkness. We tried to follow her again ; but could not keep up, and we had also outdistanced the other two ships that were following."

In the early hours of next morning, August 13th, MacFarlane saw great activity ahead, with many gun flashes and streams of coloured tracer—red, gold and pale green. An attack was being made on the convoy, and he felt far from happy, particularly as the *Melbourne Star* was, as he says, " giving a wonderful fireworks display " from her exhaust. Everything possible had been done to stop it ; but without success. As he discovered later, the activity ahead was a series of " E " boat attacks on the convoy, which did great damage. Between 1.0 and 5.0 a.m. the cruiser *Manchester* was torpedoed and sunk, as were the merchant ships *Glenorchy*, *Wairangi*, *Almeria Lykes* and *Santa Elisa*, the last two being American. The *Rochester Castle* was also hit ; but managed to proceed.

The *Melbourne Star* steamed on, keeping well away to the southward, and eventually came up to a destroyer escort. MacFarlane kept zig-zagging trying to drop in astern of one of them ; but, as he says, " none of them seemed to want us there, and we began to think we were nobody's baby and had to keep pulling away. However, just as dawn began to break I had permission from one of the destroyers to take station astern her, when another destroyer, H.M.S. *Ashanti*, came up on our starboard quarter and signalled to me to turn round and rejoin the main body of the convoy, which was astern of us. I replied ' No. I am staying where I am.' The reply came back ' I am the Admiral.' I had nothing more to say, so I turned and rejoined the convoy, which at this time consisted of the cruisers *Charybdis* and *Kenya*, followed by S.S.'s *Rochester Castle* and *Waimarama*, with the S.S. *Ohio*, which had been badly damaged, coming up astern. I took my station astern of the *Waimarama*, and shortly after this the air attacks recommenced. Some time later the S.S.'s *Dorset* and *Port Chalmers* appeared over the horizon."

Rear-Admiral Burrough's flagship, the cruiser *Nigeria*, having been hit and damaged by a torpedo, he had transferred his flag to the *Ashanti*.

Of all the Malta convoys from the west this was undoubtedly the worst of any. The attacks of the Luftwaffe were relentless and increasing, starting again at about 7.0 a.m. with many dive-bombers and torpedo-bombers. Once more the calm sea spouted with the tall greyish-white plumes as bombs fell and burst. Again the clear sky became pock-marked with the heavy black, white and golden puffs of exploding anti-aircraft shell. Occasionally, as the torpedo-bombers came skimming in low over the water, the air became criss-crossed with the red streaks of tracer from the short-range weapons, and great areas of sea were spattered with shell fragments as though from some titanic hailstorm. Each ship was in action and every gun. How many aircraft were knocked out of the sky I have no record ; but one of the first casualties on our side was the destroyer *Foresight*. Hit by a torpedo she was towed for 12 hours ; but finally had to be sunk.

The *Melbourne Star*, as we have said, had taken station astern of the *Waimarama*, a large ship heavily laden with petrol and ammunition. At 8.10 a.m. as Captain MacFarlane describes it, a covey of dive-bombers came screaming suddenly out of the sun and a stick of bombs fell on and around the *Waimarama*, which blew up with a roar and a sheet of flame with clouds of billowing smoke, to disappear in a few seconds.

" We were showered with debris from this ship," MacFarlane wrote. " A piece of plating five feet long fell on board. The base of a steel ventilator, half an inch thick and 2½ feet high, partly demolished one of our machine gun posts, a piece of angle iron at the same time narrowly missing a cadet. The sea was one sheet of fire, and as we were so close we had to steam through it. I put the helm hard a'port and had to come down from where I was on the monkey island to the bridge to save myself from being burnt. It seemed as though we had been enveloped in smoke and flames for years, although it was only minutes, otherwise the ship could not have survived. The flames were leaping mast high, indeed, air pilots reported that at times they reached 2,000 feet. The heat was terrific. The air was becoming drier every minute, as though the oxygen were being sucked out of it, as, in fact, it was. When we inspected the damage afterwards we found that nearly all the paint on the ship's sides had been burnt away, and the bottoms of the lifeboats reduced to charcoal." A few survivors from the *Waimarama* were rescued by the destroyer *Ledbury*, among them a 17-year old cadet making his first voyage.

As has been said, the *Melbourne Star* herself carried a highly inflammable and dangerous cargo. Unable to see how he could prevent his ship from being blown up Captain MacFarlane had ordered all his men to go forward, which was a wise precaution. When the fire left by the *Waimarama* had been cleared he ordered everyone back to their stations, when it was reported that 36 men were missing. " These men," he writes, " thinking that the for'rard end of the ship had been struck, and being quite certain that if they stayed on board they would be blown up, jumped over the side," which in the circumstances was not altogether unnatural. It has to be regretted that 14 lost their lives, the other 22 being rescued by a destroyer.

The air attacks continued until the early afternoon, when they suddenly ceased. Spitfires and Beaufighters from Malta appeared overhead, and shepherded by motor torpedo-boats with minesweepers on ahead, the *Melbourne Star*, *Rochester Castle* and *Port Chalmers* steamed on for Malta, while the cruisers and destroyers turned back for Gibraltar. The merchant ships entered the Grand Harbour at about 6.0 p.m., to be received by cheering crowds of people clustered on the battlements and bands playing their loudest.

The last casualty was the Federal Steam Navigation Company's *Dorset*, which was bombed and sunk at 7.0 p.m. on August 13th. The *Port Chalmers* had a surprising escape. An aircraft torpedo caught on one of her paravane wires and providentially went clear.

The *Melbourne Star* berthed with her valuable cargo intact. Twelve hours later it was found that a 6-inch shell blown skywards from the *Waimarama* had landed on the roof of Captain MacFarlane's day cabin, smashing the deck planking, embedding itself in the steel deck beneath ; but luckily not exploding. The cargo, safely delivered, brought relief to the island at a very critical period.

We left the *Brisbane Star*, Captain F. N. Riley, steaming at a bare three knots with her bows practically removed by the explosion of a torpedo. Groping her way round Cape Bon she eventually anchored off the Tunisian port of Sousse, where the French harbour authorities tried their utmost to detain her on the score that the ship was unseaworthy, which was undoubtedly the fact. But Captain Riley was not the sort of man to take the line of least resistance, so stubbornly refused to enter the harbour. Malta was his legitimate destination, and to Malta he would go. I understand that fierce arguments took place on the *Brisbane Star's* bridge before the French Harbourmaster gave way and retired defeated. Some wireless messages passed, and finally, with a satisfactory escort of Spitfires from Malta, the damaged ship steamed 200 miles and reached the harbour of Valetta with her cargo intact the day after her sister ship.

Of that convoy of 14 merchant vessels which sailed for Malta from Great Britain in August, 1942, no more than five reached their destination—the *Melbourne Star, Brisbane Star, Rochester Castle, Port Chalmers* and *Ohio*, the last-named, though arriving with portion of her oil cargo intact, being finally written off as a constructive loss. In 1943, when I was in Malta, she was serving as a fuelling jetty for destroyers. I believe she has now been towed out of harbour and sunk in deep water.

Captain David Rattray MacFarlane, of the *Melbourne Star* and Captain Frederick Nevill Riley, of the *Brisbane Star* were both awarded the Distinguished Service Order. They were among the first officers of the Merchant Navy to receive this signal honour for, in the words of the Official London Gazette :

"Fortitude, seamanship and endurance in taking Merchantmen through to Malta in the face of relentless attacks by day and night from enemy submarines, aircraft and surface forces."

The list below may not be complete ; but so far as I can ascertain from the Company's records, and protracted research in back numbers of the London Gazette, the following officers and men of the Blue Star Line were also recognized for their gallantry, resolution, skill and devotion to duty in one or other of those eventful convoys to Malta. For the comparatively few who received decorations or mentions, there were probably many more who deserved them.

DISTINGUISHED SERVICE CROSS

Mr. Leslie Parsons.	Chief Officer.	*Melbourne Star.*
Mr. R. White.	Chief Officer	*Brisbane Star.*
Mr. Harry Blandford.	Chief Engineer.	*Melbourne Star.*
Mr. Allan Ramsay Nicol.	Chief Engineer.	*Brisbane Star.*
Mr. C. R. Horton.	Second Officer.	*Brisbane Star.*
Mr. J. Dobbie.	Junior Second Engineer.	*Brisbane Star.*

DISTINGUISHED SERVICE MEDAL

Mr. Herbert O'Connor.	Chief Steward.	*Melbourne Star.*
Mr. J. Cook.	Boatswain.	*Melbourne Star.*
Mr. F. Wilson.	Boatswain.	*Brisbane Star.*
Mr. A. Nylander.	Carpenter.	*Brisbane Star.*
Mr. Frederick McWilliam	Lamptrimmer.	*Melbourne Star.*
Mr. James Fleming.	Able Seaman.	*Melbourne Star.*
Mr. Alexander Greenwood.	Able Seaman.	*Melbourne Star.*

MENTIONED IN DESPATCHES

Mr. C. W. Almond.	Chief Refrigerating Engineer.	*Melbourne Star.*
Mr. W. E. Richards.	Second Officer.	*Melbourne Star.*
Mr. G. D. Knight.	Third Officer.	*Melbourne Star.*
Mr. A. J. Pretty.	Junior Third Engineer.	*Brisbane Star.*
Mr. H. McNeilly.	Engine Room Storekeeper.	
Mr. R. Whitton.	Greaser.	

THE RELIEF OF MALTA

The M.V. "Melbourne Star," one of the few vessels to survive the convoy
battle, being welcomed at Malta on her arrival.   August 13th, 1942

CHAPTER XI

THE FREETOWN AREA AND THE ATLANTIC
August—October, 1942

VIKING STAR—August 25th
TUSCAN STAR—September 6th
ANDALUCIA STAR—October 6th
EMPIRE STAR—October 23rd
PACIFIC STAR—October 27th

I

AS has already been said, 1942 was the worst year of the U-boat war, and June, with the sinking of 135 British and Allied merchant vessels of about 680,000 gross tons, the worst month.* By August new submarines were coming from the building yards faster than we could destroy them, and as early as in May Admiral Doenitz was reporting to the Fuehrer that 124 submarines were in the operational zones—85 in the Atlantic—while another 114 new boats were in the Baltic working up for active service. The large increase in the U-boat fleet, he added, coupled with the building of submarine tankers, or " milch cows," as the Germans called them, would enable them to attack shipping in additional and more remote areas. By the use of the submarine tankers at sea the 517-ton U-boats would be able to operate for a fortnight in the Gulf of Mexico, off Panama, or as far away as off the Cameroons or Bahia ; and the larger boats off the River Plate, the Cape of Good Hope, and as far north as Mombasa in the Indian Ocean.

In June, 1942, the German Naval Staff was also planning to counter the measures taken by Brazil with a powerful blow. The fact that Brazilian aircraft were attacking Axis submarines was not the only decisive factor, it was explained to Hitler.

* If Neutral merchant vessels be included the figures are 144 ships of 700,000 tons.

Equally important was the conviction that Brazil, because of her warlike actions, was already in a virtual state of war, and was only waiting until she had made all her preparations before making the formal announcement.

During the period August, 1942, until the end of the year, the main fury of the U-boat campaign was still concentrated in the North Atlantic, where the bulk of our defence had also to be assembled. But the Germans had sufficient U-boats to carry out a sharp offensive near Trinidad and off the coast of Brazil, to catch the shipping carrying bauxite from South America to the munition factories of the United States ; in the Windward Passage, south-east of Cuba, to prey upon the shipping taking aircraft and other supplies from the United States to the Middle East round the Cape of Good Hope ; while more submarines were available for the Mediterranean, the Arctic, and in the area around Freetown, Sierra Leone. Still more were probing for " soft spots " off the Cape of Good Hope.

The range of the U-boats was constantly being extended, and with our defences stretched almost to breaking point we were having the greatest difficulty in providing the necessary long-range surface escorts and air-cover. The enemy was using his U-boats with consummate skill and flexibility, and constantly threw the concentrated venom of his onslaught on the weakest spots in our defences. No sooner had our counter-measures in any one area become really effective than the U-boats withdrew, sought for another " soft spot," and again attacked with vigour. It was impossible always to foresee where the next blow would fall. We had neither the surface craft nor the long-range aircraft to create a fully effective convoy system in each and every area to which the U-boats might penetrate.

2

VIKING STAR
August 25th, 1942

On July 30th, 1942, the *Viking Star*, a 6,400 ton steamer of the Blue Star Line commanded by Captain James Edward Mills, sailed from Buenos Ayres on her way home with 4,500 tons of frozen meat and 200 tons of fertilizer. On the afternoon of August 25th, after an uneventful voyage across the South

Atlantic, she was about 180 miles to the southward of Freetown, Sierra Leone, whence she would sail on to the United Kingdom in convoy. The visibility was good, with a fresh breeze from the south-south-west and a moderate sea.

At about 4.50 p.m. the ship was suddenly torpedoed on the port side, the explosion completely smashing two boats, inundating the main deck with water, and breaking several steam-pipes. The vessel at once listed heavily over to port, and was obviously sinking. Orders were given to abandon ship, and the two starboard lifeboats were lowered and manned and life-rafts dropped overboard. Mr. J. Rigiani, the Third Officer, described what happened.

One lifeboat, fairly full of men, cast off and drifted away from the ship, together with one raft. After procuring a sextant from the chartroom and making certain that no one was left on board, Rigiani slid down a life-line into the second boat, which also had men in it. This boat, however, was filled to the thwarts with water and useless, so most of its occupants swam to a raft nearby. The raft became over-loaded and was in danger of capsizing, so Rigiani left it and swam to another which was made fast to the other boat.

This sound boat pulled back to the damaged one, and for some time they tried to bale her out. But their efforts were useless. The second boat was completely waterlogged. Accordingly, they transferred the stores and water and cast her adrift. They were still busy about this and about half-a-mile away from the ship when she was again torpedoed. The heavy explosion broke the *Viking Star's* back. Bow and stern reared themselves out of the water and disappeared, with the red ensign still flying at the gaff.

Before she finally made off, the U-boat came to the surface and questioned survivors in the lifeboat as to the name of the ship and cargo. Her captain, who spoke some English, and was described as a big man with a red beard, boasted that he had sunk nine ships in the last four days, and that his total bag to date was 52.

Something over 30 men were in the lifeboat, in which was the Chief Officer, Mr. F. MacQuiston. Six men were on one of the rafts and seven on the other. There were two other rafts some distance away, and when dusk came the Chief Officer signalled with lights and electric torches and had replies. Up to date the weather had been calm ; but during the night the wind and sea rose and the rafts began bumping.

At daylight next morning, August 26th, both rafts were lashed together to act as a sea anchor for the lifeboat. At noon the Chief Officer raised the question of leaving the rafts together and of sailing off in the lifeboat for help. Rigiani thereupon pointed out they were in a patrol area only 150 miles from Freetown, and that they had sighted and signalled to a Sunderland flying-boat only five hours before the ship was torpedoed. He suggested that they should wait for 24 hours before separating, to which the Chief Officer agreed.

The sea rose somewhat during the day, and towards dusk their hopes were raised by sighting smoke on the horizon. Efforts were made to attract attention with smoke floats ; but they were unsuccessful.

Rigiani issued rations to the 13 men on the rafts. Preparing for the worst, he rationed the food and water to last for 25 days. It worked out at one biscuit, one spoonful of pemmican, one tablet of Horlick's malted milk, one piece of chocolate, and half a small dipper of water per man each night and morning. They had in the rafts besides the food and water, one axe, one weather cloth, a compass, an emergency light which soon ceased to function because of sea water, some smoke signals, two spoons, two dippers, a small coil of lashing, six blankets and paddles.

During the second night the crew were divided up into two six hour watches. Six men slept on the good raft, and the other seven sat on the one that was awash with the water almost up to their waists. It was cold, and they soon began to feel the effects of sitting in water.

At 6.0 next morning, August 27th, Rigiani issued rations of food and water. Meanwhile the wind and sea rose, and made life in the rafts even more difficult. The lifeboat had difficulty in keeping at a safe distance from the rafts.

The question of separating was again discussed, and after Cadet Patterson had been transferred from the raft to the boat, and Able Seaman Daintith had given up his place in the boat to Gunner Hancock, the boat sailed off and disappeared to the north-east.

Mr. MacQuiston, having transferred some stores, and a mast and large flag, to the rafts, intended to send help. It was the only seamanlike thing to be done. His boat, with a life-saving capacity of 32 people, was already overcrowded with 36. To have embarked 13 more from the rafts in the prevailing weather conditions was to risk disaster.

It blew hard on August 27th and 28th, with a heavy breaking sea. However, the boat, running before the wind, made good progress. By midnight the Chief Officer realised they must be near the land. His men were utterly exhausted when, at 3.0 a.m. on the 29th, the boat was caught in heavy surf. Three curling seas broke over her in rapid succession, and everyone was swept overboard. Men, boat and all were dashed on to a sandy beach. With what efforts one does not know they managed to haul the boat up and strip her of food and water.

It was a lonely part of the coast of Sierra Leone ; but after sundry vicissitudes MacQuiston and all his men reached safety. Of those in the lifeboat the Chief Officer made particular mention of Mr. F. Jones, the Second Officer, and Able Seaman F. Mayes who set a fine example.

Rigiani and his men, with one sound raft and the other waterlogged, finally struggled ashore on the coast of Liberia on September 4th. The story of the voyage may be told as far as possible in Rigiani's own words.

"I decided that we were making a course approximately east-south-east at about twelve to fifteen miles a day. If the wind held there would be a chance to hit land before the Guinea current swept us around the bulge of Africa and into the Gulf of Guinea. This course was materially assisted by energetic paddling to keep the wind astern. . . The knowledge that the land lay some 150 miles to the eastward was of great assistance to our spirits, despite the fact that many were suffering from open wounds and cuts, with little or no clothing to protect them from the alternate heat of the sun and the extreme chill of frequent rain squalls, and the accumulating and depressing ordeal of spending every other six hours sitting in salt water. Each morning and evening the food ration was issued and the men tackled it with gusto. Occasionally a fish was caught and then the diet was varied with raw fish. Unfortunately we could not take full advantage of the rain storms to eke out our water ration owing to the fact that our blankets and weather cloth were continually soaked in salt water."

On August 28th, with the wind continuing from the south-west, the rafts made fair progress. They spent the day keeping them stern on to the sea, replacing the lashings and wedging lifejackets between the rafts to prevent chafe. At 6.0 p.m., just before sunset, they sighted what looked like another raft about three miles to the westward. By next day all hands had settled down to watchkeeping and everyone was pulling his weight. One or two were suffering from exposure and fits of shivering, though there were no complaints. It was very cold during the ensuing night, and Rigiani issued an extra ration of malted milk tablets as some sort of compensation. August 30th :

"6.0 a.m. Food and drink. The sea was choppy but the sun broke through the cloud banks and it became quite warm. At about 8.0 a.m., we sighted smoke to the southward, and later made out the masts, funnel and finally the hull of a steamer."

They tried to attract her attention with flares and smoke signals, but to their mortification they were not seen and the vessel passed on and out of sight.

"The men were rather depressed ; but not for long. The warmth of the sun was invigorating. They stretched out as best they could and for the first time since leaving the ship felt really warm."

For the past three days the rafts had become the focus of interest to many small sharks. "Today," Rigiani writes for August 30th, " some really big ones came too close for comfort. During the day we also observed many barracuda, and once a large whale broke surface within 50 feet of the raft."— Sufficiently unnerving !

"With nightfall came wind. The sea became fiercer. We heard an aeroplane overhead during the night, but had no means of attracting attention."

At dawn on the last day of August it was blowing hard, and the vicious seas were breaking over the rafts. It was hard work to keep them running before wind and sea. Biscuits had become sodden, as the lockers, supposedly watertight, were full of water. Sea water had found its way into the tins of pemmican and chocolate. It was lucky the weather moderated during the day to a gentle breeze from the south-west with a small sea and swell. They sighted another raft about a mile away before darkness came. It was still in sight next morning, September 1st, and after four hours hard paddling, two with the available paddles and the rest with their hands, they came up with the raft and took off it a man called Boardman.

"We lashed the three rafts together and in celebration had an extra food and water ration. Our provision situation was considerably improved by the addition of the foodstuffs from the third raft. It also had red lights and Wessex flares (all useless because the tins were not watertight), and a first-aid kit was full of water. However, I managed today to dry some of the lint and bandages and apply a few dressings to Boardman who was suffering severely from salt water boils. All hands were suffering from this same painful ailment and could not bear to be touched in certain parts of their bodies. During the afternoon land was sighted far away to the eastward, and all hands paddled enthusiastically towards it for the rest of the day and during the night."

At about 2.0 a.m. heavy rainstorms set in, and when the dawn broke, dull and overcast, no land was in sight. However, as the wind and sea continued in the south-west they kept them astern and paddled on. When night came the intermittent rain ceased and the wind freshened. There was a very heavy ground swell ; but they did not mind this, as it still carried them shorewards. At about 9.0 p.m. they sighted a bright light, flashing three times every second, apparently to the south-east. They were unable to take its bearing, as the compass bowl had been carried away in the bad weather on the second night of the voyage ; but keeping the light on the starboard quarter they paddled on during the night, working in two hour watches. In between whiles they tried to snatch a little sleep, but this was practically impossible.

" September 3rd," Rigiani writes. " With daylight we observed a hump of rock, apparently an island, with a light-house on it, away to the south-east, distant about nine or ten miles. As I was afraid of slipping past this to the southward, I ordered the course to be hauled further round to the north-ward and continued paddling. At noon we cut the third raft adrift to facilitate progress. The men were now very weak from exhaustion, but they kept gamely on, and in the late afternoon we were rewarded by seeing the island recede further round to the starboard quarter, and finally at about 5.0 p.m. a line of low land broke to the eastward from north to south, distant about five miles. A double issue of food and drink put new energy into us, and we paddled on through the night. . . . At about midnight the heavy swell changed into long rollers, and I realised that we were close to the land. After another hour we suddenly heard the roar of surf and found ourselves in very heavy breakers. A dark line of land was visible ahead. We made an attempt to coast in on the breakers ; but the seas were too high and I realised that it was essential to try to keep off shore until morning. By now the breakers were continually surging over the rafts, and all hands were in danger of being washed off. After fighting our way in an attempt to get out beyond the breakers we were caught in a cross breaker and driven inshore again. Suddenly a very high breaker tossed the raft completely over and all hands were swept off. Luckily everyone managed to clamber back ;

but we lost everything except the food in the locker and some of the water. For the rest of the night we clung to the rafts and by the mercy of God were not swept by any more breakers."

When daylight came on September 4th the land was about half-a-mile away. Rigiani served out a ration of food and water, after which they broke up one of the rafts. Using bits of the floorboards as paddles they drove their other crazy craft in on the breakers and towards the shore. After an hour's hard work a breaker caught them and flung them within swimming distance of the shore. As everyone could swim, Rigiani ordered them all to take to the water and make the best of their way ashore. The beach shelved very steeply. There was a fierce undertow, and a hard fight for people to save themselves even when their feet touched the sand. As they were struggling the raft was flung in among them, and when the men finally dragged themselves ashore it was discovered that Boardman, who, it will be remembered, had been taken off the third raft some days before, was missing. They searched for him at once ; but he was never seen again.

The men were so exhausted after their ordeal that they practically collapsed in the sand. After a while some natives arrived and told the castaways they had landed in Liberia. Taken to the native village, they were given food and drink. Next morning, September 5th, they set off along the beach to the nearest town, Cape Mount, and after walking about five hours along the sand and two hours through jungle came to a village called Latia, overtaking on the way Mr. Sullivan, the Chief Radio Operator of the *Viking Star*, who had been alone on a raft until he drifted ashore.

From Latia Rigiani sent a note to a Dutch Trader at Cape Mount, and at about midnight a launch belonging to Pan-American Airways came and took them the rest of the way. Here, at the Dutch trader's house, they were treated with every hospitality and their wounds dressed. Their greatest delight, however, was to find more of the *Viking Star's* people, in the shape of the Chief and Second Engineers and one of the refrigerating greasers. Rigiani reported to the Chief Engineer as the senior officer.—" Herewith," concluded the Third Officer, " I append the full list of survivors under me this sixth day of September, 1942. Mr. P. Sullivan, First Radio Officer ; Mr. D. P. Lennon, Fourth Engineer ; T. Hewett,

Lamptrimmer ; J. Daintith, A.B. ; W. Kaye, A.B. ; E. Kitchen, A.B. ; J. Hitchin, A.B. ; P. Quirke, A.B. ; L. Lipton, Refrigerator Greaser ; C. Hill, Chief Steward ; J. Lynch, Deck-hand ; J. Holmes, Deck-hand."

Mr. Sullivan, as has been said, was alone on his raft. Reading the account of Mr. Rigiani's voyage, one cannot but think that those 11 men who were with him owed their lives to the mercy of Providence and the leadership, good sense and seamanship of their Third Officer.

The total casualties in the *Viking Star*, which included Captain Mills, were eight, one of whom Able Seaman R. Boardman, was drowned during the landing from the rafts. Most of the others, including Mr. W. Clarke, the Third Engineer, perished in the engine-room or stokehold when the ship was torpedoed.

Mr. Frederick MacQuiston, the Chief Officer, was later awarded the M.B.E. This honour was announced in the London Gazette of January 5th, 1943, with the following citation :

" The ship, when sailing alone, was torpedoed. The Chief Officer, with thirty-six men in his boat, decided to make for land and so get help for the other survivors on rafts, with whom he left three weeks supply of provisions and water. By his leadership and skill Chief Officer MacQuiston brought thirty-six people to safety, and his efforts led to the early rescue of the other survivors."

3

TUSCAN STAR
September 6th, 1942

The *Tuscan Star*, a motor-vessel of 11,400 tons, built in 1930, was in action early in the war while under the command of Captain Owen Conder Roberts, who, as captain of the *Australia Star* in 1946, was awarded the C.B.E. for long and meritorious service in the Merchant Navy.

At 3.55 p.m. on December 17th, 1939, while in the English Channel off Folkestone, the ship was suddenly attacked by a German aircraft with bombs and machine-guns. No bombs hit, thanks to Captain Roberts' zig-zagging, though one missed and exploded within 20 feet. The aircraft made three direct attacks lasting over nearly 20 minutes, and flying very low raked the ship fore and aft with machine-guns, to which the *Tuscan Star's* gunners replied with their 12-pounder. The bridge, wireless-room, boat deck and after gun platform were all hit by bullets, and Mr. T. Porteous, the Second Wireless Officer, was severely wounded in the right leg. But for the captain's evasive action and the ship's gunfire the casualties would probably have been much heavier.

On September 6th, 1942, by which date the last of the *Viking Star's* survivors were in safety, the *Tuscan Star*, then commanded by Captain Edgar Norton Rhodes, was on her homeward voyage from Buenos Ayres by way of Santos, Brazil, and Freetown. She carried 25 passengers and a crew of 88, with a heavy cargo, including 7,300 tons of frozen meat. At about 9.0 p.m., when steaming north at $13\frac{1}{2}$ knots in a position about 270 miles south of where the *Viking Star* had been sunk about 12 days before, she was suddenly torpedoed twice in quick succession on the starboard side, once in the engine-room and again in Number 5 hold.

The ship immediately started to settle rapidly by the stern and listed heavily over to starboard. Orders were at once given to abandon ship, and all boats except the motor-boat, which had been badly damaged by the explosion, were lowered, manned, and away from the ship in about 10 minutes. The ship took the final plunge and disappeared about four minutes later.

Soon afterwards the U-boat surfaced, put a small searchlight on the lifeboats, and an English-speaking officer interrogated the survivors, asking the usual questions, as to the name of the ship, what cargo she carried, where from and whither bound. The submarine came back later, her officer saying that they had rescued Mr. Gill, the Second Radio Officer, from the water and intended retaining him as a prisoner. The German, noticing women and children among the survivors, ordered the Third Officer's boat alongside, and passed down some tinned provisions. " I am sorry," he said ; " but I have to do my duty." The U-boat then gathered way and disappeared into the darkness.

A little later the Third Officer reported his boat was leaking badly and that he had no room to bale her out, whereupon he was ordered to transfer the women and children to the Captain's boat. The boats lay round the scene of the wreck during the night in good weather, but with a fairly heavy southerly swell. Some of the passengers and crew were seasick ; but at six o'clock next morning all three boats set sail, steering north in a fair southerly breeze and making good about three knots. The swell persisted ; but recovering from their seasickness, the occupants were all given their rations of water, pemmican, biscuits, chocolate and malted milk tablets. In the afternoon of that second day, September 7th, Captain Rhodes lost sight of the boats in charge of the Chief and Third Officer.

Except for the inevitable discomfort and occasional squalls with some showers of rain, the voyage of the Captain's boat was uneventful. However, they were happy when at about 3.0 p.m. they sighted a large steamer coming up from the southward, and altered course to cut her off. They were duly sighted and picked up by the Orient Liner *Otranto*, employed on Government service, at about 4.30, reaching Freetown next afternoon and Liverpool on September 25th.

The other boats also reached safety, though nine men had been lost when the *Tuscan Star* was torpedoed.

4

ANDALUCIA STAR
October 6th, 1942

On September 26th, 1942, the 15,000 tons Blue Star liner *Andalucia Star*, commanded by Captain James Bennett Hall, sailed from Buenos Ayres for the United Kingdom by way of Freetown. She carried the usual large cargo of refrigerated meat and other foodstuffs, and had on board a crew of 170 and 83 passengers, mainly British volunteers coming home to take part in the war, and including 22 women and three children. All went well until about 10.0 p.m. on the night of October 6th, when, steaming at her full speed of 16 knots without lights, in a position about 180 miles south-west of Freetown and within a few hundred miles of where the *Viking Star* and *Tuscan Star* had been sent to the bottom on August 25th and September 6th, the *Andalucia Star* was torpedoed twice almost simultaneously abreast of Numbers 5 and 6 holds. Passengers and crew at once mustered at their boat stations, and on discovering that the main engine-room was flooding fast and there was no hope of saving the ship, Captain Hall gave the order for her to be abandoned.

Without the least signs of panic, all the boats were manned

by their crews and passengers, lowered, and, with one exception, got safely away. The exception was lifeboat Number 2, the forward fall of which took charge during lowering, left her suspended by the after fall, and precipitated most of the occupants and her gear into the sea. All but two of her people, Mrs. L. A. Green, a stewardess, and a steward, were rescued.

About 20 minutes after the first attack the *Andalucia Star* was torpedoed a third time. The torpedo struck on the port side abreast Number 1 hold, the detonation being so violent that it blew out the starboard side of the ship also. Two boats filled with people that were alongside the starboard side had providential escapes from being destroyed ; but were able to cast off and get clear.

Captain Hall was now left on board with four men. As the sea round the bows was covered with oil fuel, the captain took these four aft, where he hoped the water would be clearer. There he met a passenger, who, for one reason or another, had not gone to his boat station and seemed to be dazed. They managed to launch a raft and jumped overboard after it. One member of the crew, who with great difficulty had to be helped by the others, died of heart failure. The unfortunate passenger, though they searched for him, was never seen again.

At about 10.25 p.m. the *Andalucia Star* plunged to the bottom. No signs of the U-boat had been seen.

The people in the boats and raft were sorted out, and Captain Hall decided they should remain together during the night. Luckily the weather was good, with no more than a slight swell. No ships or aircraft being in sight next morning, October 7th, the boats hoisted their sails and proceeded for Freetown, about 180 miles to the north-east. Keeping together, they sailed throughout that day with a fair wind and an overcast sky with rain, until, in the early hours next morning, they sighted, and were sighted by, the corvette H.M.S. *Petunia*. By about 4.0 a.m. the occupants of all the boats had been safely picked up and were landed at Freetown the same evening.

Captain Hall was a man of few words. His report was terse and restrained, and mentioned little beyond the bare facts. But at the end of his narrative he wrote :

" I would like to mention here that W. S. Wheeler, Lamptrimmer, dived into the water from his boat and rescued a little girl passenger bringing her safely to the boat. Also N. Bennett, who volunteered to take over the wheel in place of Williams, who was a married man. This request I granted, and he was one of the last to leave the ship with me."

Captain Hall and Able Seaman Norman Bennett were both officially " commended for their services when the *Andalucia Star* was sunk, as was the Fourth Engineer, Mr. John William Hubbard, for his promptitude and devotion to duty in stopping the engines and remaining in the engine-room until ordered to leave. Mrs. L. A. Green, Stewardess, also received a posthumous commendation, the Merchant Navy equivalent of a " mention in despatches." As already mentioned, Mrs. Green lost her life during the lowering of one of the boats. She had previously shown coolness, foresight and devotion to duty in caring for the women and children passengers. One of her last acts was to switch on the red waistcoat light of a little girl aged four-and-a-half, and it was this light burning that enabled the child to be found and saved after she had been thrown into the water. When the child was in the water she was seen for an instant by a fellow passenger, but then drifted away.

For saving the life of this little girl William Stewart Wheeler, the Lamptrimmer, was awarded the Bronze Medal for Gallantry in Saving Life at Sea. I will quote the official citation from the London Gazette :

" The ship, carrying a number of passengers, was torpedoed in the darkness. As the vessel was sinking rapidly abandonment was ordered. During the abandonment one of the boats was up-ended and its occupants thrown into the sea. Other boats which had got clear were picking up survivors when the cry of a small child was heard some distance away. Wheeler immediately dived into the water, swam through wreckage for a distance of about 600 yards to the child and supported it for over 30 minutes until they were found by another boat and picked up. Lamptrimmer Wheeler displayed great courage in plunging overboard into a choppy sea covered with wreckage. But for his gallant action the life of the child would undoubtedly have been lost."

5

EMPIRE STAR
October 23rd, 1942

The escape of the *Empire Star* from Singapore in February, 1942, has already been described. In October, still under the command of Captain Capon, she sailed from Liverpool with 19 passengers and a mixed cargo, including some ammunition and aircraft. Being a comparatively fast ship she was routed independently far out in the Atlantic, and sailed unescorted. There had been some changes among the officers. Mr. Dawson, the Chief Officer at the time of her escape from Singapore, had been relieved by Mr. L. Vernon, while Mr. J. P. Smith had been promoted from Third Officer to Second. The new Third Officer was Mr. R. Moscrop-Young.

On the afternoon of October 23rd the ship was almost in mid-Atlantic about 570 miles north of the Azores steaming southerly at 14 knots. There was a clear sky with good visibility, and it was blowing hard from the north-west with a heavy swell and breaking sea. To prevent damage to the valuable deck cargo, zig-zagging had been discontinued.

At 3.43 p.m., a torpedo struck and exploded the starboard side amidships, Mr. Vernon actually hearing the thud of its impact a split second before the roar of the detonation. The engine-room was immediately flooded, which stopped the ship and put out the lights. Two engineers and two others on duty below were killed immediately, while two more men on the upper platform of the engine-room were injured.

The ship listed heavily over to starboard. Passengers and crew assembled at their boat stations. There were originally four lifeboats; but one, on the starboard side, had been destroyed by the explosion. Orders were given to abandon ship, which, in spite of the heavy sea, was carried out in an orderly manner.

As the boats lay off, the ship righted herself, and, though low in the water, did not appear to be sinking. Indeed, thinking she might be saved, Mr. Vernon had the idea of returning on board to see what could be done. But about half-an-hour after the first explosion she was torpedoed again twice at five minute intervals on the starboard side aft. The *Empire Star's* stern rapidly became submerged, and flinging her bows skywards she disappeared from sight in a little up-heaval of spray and a cloud of steam and smoke, which was soon dispersed by the tearing wind. Some minutes after the ship sank, those in the boats heard and felt a heavy underwater explosion, which was sufficiently severe to cause anxiety as to their safety. It may have been caused by an explosion in the *Empire Star*; but it was peculiar that no sign of the U-boat was seen either before or after the torpedoing. It was the usual habit of the German submarine commanders to surface and to question the survivors as to the name of the ship and the cargo carried.

Before darkness came Mr. Vernon picked up five survivors who were floating about on rafts, which brought the complement of his boat to 34. Her official life-saving capacity was 40 ; but even with six less the Chief Officer found his boat inconveniently crowded and difficult to handle in the heavy, breaking sea. He spoke to the two other boats, to learn that all on board the *Empire Star* except the four killed in the engine-room were accounted for. Captain Capon's orders were to keep together during the night, and then make sail for the Azores.

Throughout the hours of darkness the wind still raged furiously and the curling, breaking seas came surging down from the north-west. Those in the boats were drenched with spray and bitterly cold. As Mr. Vernon wrote :

"We lay to a sea anchor during the night ; but in addition to the sea anchor we had to use five oars to keep the boat's head to sea and avoid flooding. I tried to communicate with the other boats by light ; but was unsuccessful."

Any seaman can visualize what lay behind the Chief Officer's simple description : those plunging, crowded boats with the spray sweeping over them in sheets ; the alternate roar and lull of the gale as they rose to the foaming crests and fell dizzily into the troughs ; the sickening motion ; and the constant watchfulness as the labouring men tugged at the oars to prevent broaching to and destruction.

After a miserable night, the first streaks of dawn on September 24th came stealing up over the heaving horizon to the eastward. Mr. Vernon could see no other boats when full daylight came. He hoisted his sails and steered off before the wind, until, at 10.10 a.m. :

"A boat which I have since learned was the Third Officer's " (Mr. Moscrop-Young)—" was sighted several miles distant and to the south-west. I attempted to close ; but could not steer a closing course, and at 12.30 I gave up the attempt and steered south-east."

Here, unhappily, it has to be said that Captain Capon's boat, in which were 38 people, was never seen again. Mr. Moscrop-Young had tried to take his boat alongside the Captain's to take off some of his people soon after the ship was abandoned. But in the heavy sea he was unable to do so. They had six oars out ; but found it impossible to pull up to windward. Of what happened to Captain Capon's boat we have no knowledge, and can only surmise. As Mr. Vernon wrote :

> " If for any reason a boat got beam on to the sea for two or three successive heavy seas I consider that in the conditions prevailing she could easily have capsized."

To continue Mr. Vernon's story. By 5.0 p.m. on the 24th the sea and swell had become so heavy that he was forced to lower the sail and lie to a sea anchor during the night, oars again being used to keep the boat head to sea. At 11.0 p.m. the rudder broke off at the top pintle and was useless. They had to use a steering oar instead, at best a cumbrous expedient. The weather was as wild as ever at daylight on the 25th, so, as he writes :

> " We drifted before the wind with sail and sea anchor until picked up by H.M.S. *Black Swan* at 6.15 p.m."

Radio signals of distress had been sent off from the *Empire Star* on being torpedoed. The Third Officer's boat was also picked up by the *Black Swan*. To those wireless messages, and to the fine seamanship of Mr. Vernon, the Chief Officer ; Mr. Moscrop-Young, the Third Officer ; and all those others who helped them in those hours of trial, must be attributed the fact that so many people of the *Empire Star* were brought to safety, when so many might have perished.

Mr. W. A. Smith, one of the passengers of the *Empire Star* wrote to the Blue Star Line :

> " I cannot fully enjoy the feeling of safety without making comments on the behaviour of your officers and men at the recent disaster—Chief Officer Vernon and Second Officer Smith upheld the true traditions of the Merchant Navy. These officers worked with unflinching courage throughout. The boat was handled with skill in fearful weather. Both officers never tired in their fight for our lives. They always had words of encouragement for their passengers.—I would like also to make special mention of Mr. Donaldson A.B. This man worked like a Trojan throughout our ordeal. The excellent radio service on board certainly set the rescue machine in motion, but I feel certain that Messrs. Vernon and Smith were very largely responsible for our salvation. To these fine officers I say thank you, and may God grant them their reward in the trying days ahead of us."

That fine tribute is borne out by another passenger, Mr. W. F. Blackhall, who wrote :

> " I should like to place on record that I consider I owe my life to the seamanship, courage and tact of Chief Officer Vernon, most ably backed up by Second Officer Smith. Seaman Donaldson was outstanding among the members of the crew of the lifeboat for the energy and zeal with which he obeyed all orders."

" MELBOURNE STAR "

Discharging war supplies at Malta.   August 1942.

One of the people in Mr. Moscrop-Young's boat was Lieutenant Raymond Percival Atkinson, R.N.R., himself a Master Mariner. Writing of the Third Officer, he says :

" He was in charge of our lifeboats, and showed remarkable coolness, ability and seamanship in the handling and management of same, and I cannot speak too highly of him and think this officer will go far in his career. I wish him every success. I would also like to mention assistance given by Mr. Hickman, Junior Engineer, whose help was continuous and unending."

These unsolicited eulogies to bravery and fine seamanship were fully deserved, and it is pleasant to know that the services of Mr. L. Vernon, the Chief Officer, and Mr. R. Moscrop-Young were both officially recognised by the award of the M.B.E. Able Seaman I. H. Donaldson received a well-merited British Empire Medal.

6

PACIFIC STAR
October 27th, 1942

On October 18th, 1942, the *Pacific Star*, Captain G. L. Evans, sailed from Freetown in company with a large convoy of about 40 other ships and an escort of five corvettes. On the afternoon of the 27th, when about 170 miles to the westward of the Canary Islands, the convoy Commodore signalled to all his ships that U-boats were known to be in the vicinity. The convoy at the time was on a broad front of 11 columns, of which the *Pacific Star* led the eighth.

At 5.30 p.m., as a result of the submarine warning, the mean course of the convoy was altered 30 degrees to starboard. Two hours later, by which time it was dark, the convoy swung back to the original mean course. The U-boats must have been present in some numbers, for almost at once the *Pacific Star* was torpedoed forward on the starboard side, just about the centre of Number 1 hatch. The violent explosion blew hatches and cargo into the air, and buckled and burst open the deck plating. The ship next astern of the *Pacific Star* was also torpedoed and set on fire.

The weather at the time was good, and for a time Captain Evans steamed on with the convoy, though gradually losing speed because of the hole in his bows. He hoped to be able to carry on ; but during the night the wind and sea rose until it was blowing a gale from the worst quarter, the north-west. Forced again to ease down to reduce the strain on his damaged bows and bulkheads, Captain Evans saw that the convoy was gradually drawing ahead and leaving him. Conditions were rapidly becoming worse as the wind freshened. They trimmed the tanks in an effort to keep the ship up forward ; but it did little good. By 2.0 a.m. next morning, October 28th, it being bright moonlight, the convoy was completely out of sight. Soon afterwards he realised the *Pacific Star* was a straggler, and gave up all hope of catching up. No assistance was forthcoming. Indeed, with such a slender escort for a large convoy, it is difficult to see how help could have been given without endangering other ships. The *Pacific Star* was alone, and as she was gradually settling down by the head Captain Evans altered course to the eastward for Gibraltar. This brought wind and sea on the port beam.

By 3.30 a.m. the weather was too bad to steer for Gibraltar. Captain Evans had no alternative but to turn and make for the Canary Islands, thus bringing the sea right astern. Even so, with a full gale and a heavy, toppling sea the *Pacific Star* made very heavy weather of it, one of the after lifeboats being smashed and torn away from its falls.

The ship struggled gamely on, the captain and crew doing all they could to save her. But at 5.0 p.m. the bulkhead to Number 2 hold, abaft the hold that had been damaged, was heard to collapse. The ship was becoming unmanageable. The water in Number 2 hold was up to 22 feet, though three pumps were kept on it. The ship was gradually sinking by the bows. Captain Evans and his officers and men, consummate seamen though they were, could do no more. It was now, towards dusk, that it was decided to abandon ship. The commercial S.O.S. wireless signal was sent out several times ; the boats were lowered, and officers and crew left the ship. They had orders to remain close to the vessel through the night.

Captain Evans says nothing in his report of what happened during the hours of darkness ; but when the stormy dawn came grey and leaden over the sea on October 29th, his own and the Second Officer's boat were the only ones near the wreck or in sight of each other. The Captain still had hopes that his ship might be saved if any vessel had heard the S.O.S. radio signals and arrived to take the *Pacific Star* in tow. But no ship hove up over the wind-swept horizon as they rose on the foaming crests—nothing. It was impossible to re-board the stricken ship, which lay waterlogged and helpless. The great seas were bursting over her weather side, and pouring off her in cascades to leeward.

No man could do more than those men did. They stuck by their stricken ship all day, and all through the next night, in the dwindling hope that another vessel would arrive to save a valuable cargo.

"The morning of the 30th," Captain Evans wrote, "the weather was still bad, the ship listing heavily to port, against all portside tanks being empty. She was waterlogged and had ceased to drift. With the foredeck awash we were unable to get back against the gale, and in view of the condition of the men in the boats we had to leave her and make for the land. The vessel was settling down as we left."

And there, in his terse and abrupt manner of writing, Captain Evan's story ends. He tells us nothing of where he and his men landed, or what they must have experienced during a tempestuous and most uncomfortable voyage.

All we know is that every officer and man of the *Pacific Star* survived to fight again, and that Captain G. L. Evans was subsequently awarded the O.B.E. for his gallant efforts to bring a valuable ship and her cargo to safety.

I have discovered, however, that Captain Evans wrote a glowing tribute to his First Wireless Officer, Mr. J. D. Dempster, who was officially " commended " for his services. Captain Evans said that Mr. Dempster :

"Stood by me throughout, returned to the wireless room just before we finally abandoned ship to send out the S.O.S., and was most useful to me in the boat and when we landed. He was a great help to me all the time, and was a fine fellow."

CHAPTER XII

I

ESCAPE OF THE *EMPIRE GLADE*
November 28th, 1942

IN the early hours of November 28th, 1942, the Blue Star Company's *Empire Glade*, Captain George Marmion Duff, was in a position about 840 miles north-eastward of Trinidad, zig-zagging on her course. There was a light easterly breeze with a slight sea and swell, a half-moon overhead and a partially overcast sky, with moderate visibility.

At 4.53 a.m. a submarine on the surface which was never seen, but must have sighted the *Empire Glade* in the light of the moon and the growing dawn, opened fire from a position about two points on the port bow. Her first two rounds missed; but a third hit a life-raft and ignited a number of red flares, which made the *Empire Glade* a still more conspicuous target, and also carried away the main wireless aerial.

The ship, meanwhile, had started to turn away to present her stern to the U-boat. Her officers and men had rushed to their action stations. She mounted a 4-inch gun in the stern.

The submarine fired about 10 more rounds, a fourth shell bursting in the wheelhouse, cutting electric light circuits, and causing the morse lamp on the bridge to flicker continuously. Successive hits penetrated the hull in various other places— two in Number 2 hold near the waterline; one in Number 3 'tween deck; one in the engine-room close to the waterline; and another in Number 5 lower hold.

The gunlayer, Able Seaman C. Turner, fired a round from his gun towards the unseen enemy. But accurate shooting was impossible. All Turner could do was to shoot at the flash of the U-boat's gun on the off-chance of getting somewhere near. Then, at 5.3 a.m., as the result of the hit in the engine-room, the *Empire Glade's* engines suddenly stopped. At that moment she must have seemed doomed, and would undoubtedly have been sunk if the Chief and Second Engineers, Messrs. J. B. Parker and D. C. Keenliside, had not gone below and got the engines running again. In five minutes the ship was again on the move, and a little later was travelling at full speed. Turner, the gunlayer in the stern, had used his initiative by starting a smoke screen, which made the ship a more difficult target and helped her to escape.

From first to last the U-boat was never sighted, and in the course of the short engagement the *Empire Glade's* cabin boy had been killed and five men wounded. But with that single fatal casualty the ship, with her remaining crew of 47, succeeded in making her escape.

Some people, with their ship badly hit and her engines out of action for the time being, might have been tempted to throw up the sponge. But Captain Duff and his people were of different mettle, and for his great bravery and devotion to duty the Captain was awarded the George Medal and Lloyds War Medal for Bravery at Sea.

In his report the Captain specially mentioned the following : Chief Engineer J. B. Parker and Second Engineer D. C. Keenliside for their devotion to duty in going below under heavy fire and re-starting the engines at a very critical moment ; Chief Officer G. Roberts and Second Officer A. C. Hender for their devotion to duty, courageous bearing and fine organization and leadership throughout the action ; Able Seaman C. Turner, for devotion to duty, efficient leadership and organization of his gun's crew, and for his initiative in lighting the smoke screen and helping the ship to escape ; Carpenter H. Shakeshaft and Engine-Room Storekeeper F. Simmons, for their devotion to duty and excellent work, willingly and cheerfully carried out, which in great measure enabled the ship to continue on her voyage.

The official London Gazette of June 8th, 1943, announced the award of the George Medal to Captain George Marmion Duff, who had already been presented with Lloyds War Medal for Bravery at Sea. The Chief Engineer, Mr. John Bell Parker was awarded the O.B.E. ; while the Chief Officer, Second Officer and Second Engineer, Messrs. Glyn Roberts, Francis Charles Hender and Dugald Charles Keenliside received the M.B.E. Harry Shakeshaft and Frank Simmons received the British Empire Medal. The citation read :

" The ship was sailing alone when she was attacked by an enemy submarine shortly before dawn. Many shells exploded on or near the ship which, however, put up a splendid and successful defence. The vessel sustained considerable damage, but emergency repairs were effected and the ship kept going. The submarine continued to shell the ship, but the fire was returned and the enemy was eventually shaken off. In spite of the damaged condition the vessel continued her voyage and arrived at her destination after having covered a distance of over 2,500 miles.

The Master displayed great courage and skill in conducting this magnificent defence which saved his ship. It was due to his tenacity, resource and seamanship that the ship was brought safely to port.

The Chief and Second Engineers remained below throughout the attack and carried out their duties with courage and coolness despite damage caused by a shell which penetrated the engine-room.

The Chief Officer was the mainstay of the Master on deck and was outstanding in his courage and devotion to duty.

The Second Officer was the gunnery officer in the ship and it was mainly due to his excellent control and direction that such an effective fire was maintained.

The Carpenter and Storekeeper worked with courage, skill and untiring energy in effecting emergency repairs while the ship was in action."

2

THE WRECK OF THE *DUNEDIN STAR*
November 29th, 1942

NOTE :—The material from which the following account is compiled is derived from a book " Skeleton Coast " by Mr. John H. Marsh, first published in November 1944, by Messrs. Hodder and Stoughton. For security reasons, and at the request of the Admiralty, the name of the wrecked liner was then withheld. I am greatly indebted to Mr. Marsh and his Publishers for allowing me to make use of his narrative for the purposes of this book. No war history of the Blue Star Line would be complete without some account of the unfortunate wreck of the *Dunedin Star* and the rescue of the passengers and crew, which Mr. Marsh rightly describes as " one of the most remarkable rescues of modern times " in which the rescuers, " pitting themselves against the forces of Nature, overcoming one misfortune after another, carrying on with unflagging determination when the odds seemed hopeless," brought to safety every one of the more than 100 castaways marooned on an inhospitable, barren coast hundreds of miles away from the nearest civilization.

Those who want the full details of the shipwreck and all that happened, and at the same time a thrilling story of modern adventure which cost " two lives, nearly £100,000 worth of material, a tug, an aircraft, some trucks, and the expenditure of almost limitless brawn, sweat and courage on the part of some hundreds of people," are recommended to read " Skeleton Coast " in its entirety.

TAFFRAIL.

Late on the night of Sunday, November 29th, 1942, the operator of the radio station at Walvis Bay heard a distress signal coming in through his earphones. He acknowledged it, to hear that the 11,000 ton Blue Star liner *Dunedin Star* had struck a submerged object nearly 400 miles along the coast to the northward just after 10.30 p.m., had severely damaged herself, and was steaming for the coast at full speed to beach herself before she sank. The position she gave was Latitude 18°13′S., Longitude 11°55′E.

The *Dunedin Star* had sailed from Liverpool three weeks before and was on her way to the Middle East with military stores with Capetown as her first port of call. She carried more than 100 people, of whom 21 were passengers, including some women and children. Most of them were in bed or preparing to turn in when the vessel struck. Feeling the shock they left their bunks and put on warm clothing, mustering at the foot of the companion with their lifebelts. There was natural anxiety; but nothing akin to panic. Then, when the ship seemed to be moving on quite normally at her usual speed, and word came below that the passengers should return to their cabins, all seemed well.

Nothing had been seen beforehand by the officer of the watch or any of the lookouts on the bridge. All they had felt was a heavy bump, followed by two slighter bumps and shuddering as the bottom of the ship ground over something hard. She heeled over a little, and then drove on at full speed.

For some reason, possibly due to an unexpected current, the ship seems to have hit the Clan Alpine shoal, three to five miles off the coast of the Kaokoveld, South West Africa, just north of Cape Frio and some 40 miles south of the frontier with Angola.

The Captain's first reaction was to alter course out to sea. Then, within a few minutes, he had reports of the damage, which was serious enough. Part of the keel below the engine-room had been ripped away and the engine-room was leaking. Water was coming into the shaft tunnel and rising in Numbers 2 and 3 holds. The pumps were not going; but it was soon obvious that the ship was doomed. The water was gradually creeping up over the engine-room floor plates, and squirting in through the joints of the watertight doors separating the engine-room from the flooded shaft tunnel, the doors actually bulging under the pressure behind them.

The Chief Engineer, who had rushed at once to the engine-room, calculated that the *Dunedin Star* might float another three or four hours, certainly no longer. He went to the bridge and reported to the Captain, who swung the ship round until she was heading eastward, towards the land. Rather than allow his ship to sink in deep water, he had decided to beach her, which would give him a greater chance of saving the passengers and crew and might allow some of the valuable cargo to be salved. The signal of distress had already gone out and been acknowledged.

The night was pitch dark, with an overcast sky and no moon or stars. The sea was moderately calm with a long oily swell. The Captain was in a difficult position. The ship was sinking fast, and must be beached soon. But he did not know what sort of a coast he might find. If he carried on too long he might bump over more reefs and tear the bottom right out of the ship, or even crash head on into cliffs. The echo-sounding gear had been damaged and was out of action.

However, after steaming for 40 minutes breakers were sighted ahead. The water seemed to be shoaling fast, so speed was reduced. A few minutes later the vessel took the sandy beach gently and swung broadside on to the surf, heeling over to starboard towards the breaking seas. It was only just in time. The water was well over the engine-room floor plates.

Feeling the second bump as the ship took the ground the passengers again came out with their lifebelts. They were told to stand by and keep calm. There was no immediate danger. Nothing could be done until daylight.

Occasional seas were breaking and washing over the after well-deck, and down below in the engine-room the men were fighting a losing battle with the encroaching water. The pumps could not compete with the inflow, and at 20 minutes past midnight, an hour after the ship had grounded for the second time, the engine-room had to be evacuated. The *Dunedin Star* was a motor vessel. All of her pumps and auxiliary machinery were electrical, and when the engine-room was abandoned all the lights went out.

Shuddering to the impact of the heavy surf, the ship lay helpless in her sandy bed. When the clouds dispersed a gleam of moonlight shone upon ridge upon ridge of crested white surf breakers surging towards the low shore. When the dawn came struggling out of the eastern sky, those on board looked eagerly towards the land to discover what sort of a place they had come to. There was nothing much to be seen, merely that area of leaping surf rolling and breaking remorselessly against a sandy beach with a line upon line of rolling sand dunes beyond it. No vegetation was visible, no trees, shrubs or even grass, nothing but miles of those hillocks of gleaming white sand picked out here and there by rocky boulders.

Working with their auxiliary batteries the radio operators had been in further conversation with Walvis Bay. A tug and a trawler would be sent to the *Dunedin Star's* assistance ; but could not arrive for two days. What other help was needed, Walvis Bay asked ? The Captain replied that he needed assistance to get his passengers and crew on shore. The *Dunedin Star* was waterlogged. There was no knowing how long she would last.

The ship's S.O.S., meanwhile, had been relayed to all and sundry. A British freighter, the *Manchester Division*, and a Norwegian motor-vessel, the *Temeraire*, had been diverted to the scene of the wreck to try to take off the passengers, and would arrive in about 48 hours. The minesweeper H.M.S.A.S. *Nerine*, an ex-trawler, was being sent from Walvis Bay, together with the tug *Sir Charles Elliott*.

Meanwhile, on board the ship on November 30th, the coming of daylight had not alleviated the anxiety. Sandbanks had begun to form on both sides amidships, while the current was gradually sweeping away the sand from the bow and stern, which left them unsupported. The ship was rolling, bumping and straining, and might easily break her back. So the Captain decided to land his passengers and crew in the motorboat. No crowded pulling boat could have been handled in the heavy surf. She must have capsized. So the motor-boat was stocked with extra provisions, manned and lowered. They made fast a light hawser in the wreck, and the boat paid it out fathom by fathom as she approached the beach. After something of a hair-raising experience in the surf, the first boatload of passengers got safely ashore with nothing worse than a thorough drenching.

So far, so good ; but after the first people had been landed the pintles and gudgeons of the motor-boat's rudder were smashed and new ones had to be made. This meant delay. The first consignment of the crew were then ordered ashore ;

but because time was drawing on they had no chance to collect their belongings, and reached the beach with nothing more than what they had on. A third trip was safely accomplished and then, by a stroke of misfortune, the motor-boat was disabled in the heavy surf and flung shattered on the beach, useless for any further operations. No one was hurt; but this left 63 people, including eight women, three children in arms and some elderly men on the open beach without shelter, with only the food and water in the motor-boat, and no likelihood of help reaching them for at least two days. Forty-three more officers and men were left on board the *Dunedin Star*, which was slowly being battered and pounded to pieces 500 yards out in the surf.

The Chief Officer was in charge of the beach party, and immediately on landing he established some sort of a camp under the lee of a sand dune about 200 yards from the water's edge. They used the spars and sails of the abandoned motor-boat to improvise tents for as many of the women and children as they would accommodate, and carried up the food and water. The fine sand was an abomination. Stirred up by the breeze, it lodged in people's eyes, nostrils and throats.

Some groups of men went off to look for water. There was no water anywhere; but one party, going south, came upon a great spar standing upright, and the rotted, disintegrated timbers of some sailing ship wrecked years before. Nearby they found some rude plank huts, half-buried in the drifting sand. There were relics of human occupation—a vice; the remains of what seemed to be a wooden bucket, which crumbled to powder when they handled it; a book; an earthenware inkwell; some old shoes. Deeper still they came upon human bones, then upon human skeletons, complete but for the skulls. Their presence was a mystery, though it was later discovered that the remains of the ship, the huts, and the skeletons had been seen 60 years before. However, the presence of those human remains was not a happy augury. The castaways were marooned in one of the loneliest parts of the world which is almost uninhabited. They were hundreds of miles from the nearest civilization, miles upon miles of sand and arid mountains with nothing in the shape of roads.

At dusk on December 1st, the Norwegian motor-vessel *Temeraire* arrived on the scene and anchored within three miles of the wrecked *Dunedin Star*. She was followed by the

Manchester Division during the night, and the next morning the *Temeraire's* motor-boat was lowered. Manned by a volunteer crew it approached the wreck. The swell and surf were as heavy as ever. There was considerable risk, for at the moment the boat was well over the level of the *Dunedin Star's* main deck, and the next was far down in the trough. However, 10 men were embarked on that first trip and taken to the *Manchester Division*, while all the remainder of the 43 originally left on board were rescued during the morning, the Captain, Chief Engineer and another Engineer being taken to the tug *Sir Charles Elliott*, which had arrived in the meanwhile. The *Dunedin Star's* last wireless messages, sent off on her nearly exhausted auxiliary batteries, went out at 10.55 a.m.

The minesweeper *Nerine* arrived that afternoon, December 2nd, but the swell was still too heavy for much to be done. Meanwhile the *Sir Charles Elliott* was running short of coal. After transferring the Captain and the engineers to the *Nerine*, she had to return towards Walvis Bay, more than 350 miles to the southward, to obtain a further supply. As all the people had now been rescued from the *Dunedin Star* there was nothing more for the *Temeraire* to do, so she also weighed her anchor and disappeared, leaving the *Manchester Division* and *Nerine* on the scene.

Meanwhile the castaways ashore were in a bad way. Scorched by the burning sun by day, chilled to the marrow by night by the wind and drenched by the heavy dew, they had no adequate shelter, and insufficient blankets or other coverings to go round. Food and water were scarce, and all were hungry and thirsty. Moreover, the fine sand blown everywhere by the wind had become worse than a nuisance. The ship's Surgeon, Doctor Burn Wood, the oldest man in the party, did excellent work. So did a Doctor Labio, an Egyptian eye specialist. Many people were suffering from severe sunburn, and the three babies, in particular, through the fine, gritty sand in their eyes. It was a miserable sort of a picnic, and everyone who thought about it realised there was no hope of their salvation from the sea so long as the thundering surf persisted. For all they knew it might last for weeks.

But the *Manchester Division* had been communicating with Walvis Bay by wireless, and late that afternoon, December 2nd, she flashed a cheering message to the shore party. A bomber was being sent up from Capetown, 1,000 miles away, to drop supplies. Another rescue party was coming overland from Windhoek, nearly 600 miles distant by the route they would have to take.

But what a route! Most of it was through unexplored country ; the first 200 miles over an apology for a road, the next 200 over a native track through scrub and tall grass, and the last lap through untracked desert and sand-dunes between the gaunt mountains with few water-holes. However, this rescue party started off on the evening of December 2nd. There were eight vehicles in the convoy, including troop-carriers, a repair van, water trailer and ambulance. They took with them a doctor, medical supplies, water and rations.

On the morning of December 3rd, the *Nerine*, coming as close in as she dared, tried floating rafts ashore laden with food and water. The efforts were useless. Carried off by the current the rafts disappeared in the breakers to the northward.

The bomber, piloted by Captain Naude, of the Royal South African Air Force, left Capetown soon after daylight on December 3rd and reached Walvis Bay in time for the midday meal. Taking off again early in the afternoon the 'plane flew on up the coast, suddenly to see, some 40 miles short of the *Dunedin Star's* position, a small ship aground in the breakers with the great seas washing over her. It was indeed, the tug *Sir Charles Elliott*, which had gone ashore at 6.0 a.m. We cannot dwell upon her misadventures, except to say that she became a total loss and that two of her men were drowned in the surf while trying to get ashore.

Flying on up the coast Naude sighted the wreck of the *Dunedin Star* and the castaways camp ashore. Running in over the camp at very low altitude he started dropping supplies. Some of the first tins of water dropped burst on landing ; but later, from no more than 20 feet, he dropped medical supplies and all manner of food in cases. From 100 feet, in parachutes, 40 gallons of fresh water landed in safety.

Naude now decided to land, with the object of taking the women and children back by air. He circled round for some time looking for a likely spot, finally to find a stretch of fairly level sand two miles inland from the camp. He landed in safety, only to find, when he tried to taxi back to take off against the strong breeze, that the 12-ton aircraft was hopelessly bogged in the soft sand. The crew did all they could with the help of five men of the *Dunedin Star* who had hurried to the spot.

124

The 'plane could not be budged. The pilot used almost the last of the power in his batteries to warn Walvis Bay by radio that the castaways from the *Dunedin Star* were in bad shape ; that his own 'plane was out of action and immovable without outside assistance—in short, that the situation was as bad as it possibly could be. The *Dunedin Star's* people on shore had some more water and provisions ; but the crew of the aircraft, four in all, were now castaways as well. Further south down the coast was the wrecked *Sir Charles Elliott.* Something also had to be done to help the 17 men on board her.

On December 4th, short of fuel, provisions and water, the *Nerine* had to sail for Walvis Bay, leaving the castaways alone and perforce taking the *Dunedin Star's* Captain and two engineers with her. The Captain would have preferred to be put ashore ; but that was absolutely impossible through the heavy surf. Before sailing, however, the *Nerine* had made another attempt to float food and water ashore on an improvised raft and in some watertight containers. They were dropped overboard and carried off by the current, and as the *Nerine* slowly disappeared to the southward, the airmen, with some of the *Dunedin Star's* crew, walked northward along the beach keeping abreast of the floating raft in the hope it would be washed ashore. They were not disappointed. After drifting for nearly six miles some eddy or freakish current cast the raft on to the beach. Close by, too, they found the other rafts that had been dropped the day before. They discovered several drums of fresh water too heavy to be carried ; but found some five-gallon tins of water, some packages of bully beef and biscuit, some canvas which would be invaluable for making shelters. All they could carry they humped back to the camp. They arrived exhausted ; but what with this extra provender from the sea and that dropped by the aircraft the ration for the evening meal was increased to a tin of bully beef between two people, ship's biscuits, and a cup of tea with condensed milk and sugar. They made a fire of driftwood, of which there was plenty. The hot food and drink was a godsend, and so was the warmth of the blazing bonfire after dark.

It is unnecessary here to tell the story in all its detail ; but late on December 4th another minesweeper, the *Natalia*, left Walvis Bay for the wreck. As her wireless, like the *Nerine's* had a range of no more than 200 miles, they took the precaution of taking carrier pigeons. Another bomber left Capetown on

December 5th for Walvis Bay, and after loading up with food, water, blankets and a tent for the castaways, flew on to the northward. By about 4.30 p.m. she was over the wreck of the *Sir Charles Elliott* dropping supplies to her men on the beach. Due to lack of other containers the fresh water had been pumped into the inner tubes of motor cars. Unfortunately they burst on landing and the water was lost. The same thing happened when the 'plane dropped supplies to the castaways camp further north. The parachute of the water container failed to open, and the container split on impact. There was little better luck with the tins and packages of food, though the tent and blankets reached the ground in safety.

On Sunday, December 6th, the *Natalia* reached the wreck and dropped some further rafts with food and water for the castaways. This time there was better luck, and one raft at least drifted safely ashore and its contents were recovered. The aircraft from Walvis Bay made a second trip with supplies for the camp ; but had no success with the water in the inner tubes, which split on landing. The *Natalia*, meanwhile, which had gone south to look for some place sheltered from the surf where it might be possible to get people ashore, had developed leaking boiler tubes. After anchoring for six hours for her engineers to do what they could, she steamed back to the camp, dropped a floating drum of water overboard, and then had to shape course for Walvis Bay, signalling before she went that another vessel would be sent to the rescue.

Matters were really becoming serious when on December 7th the little *Nerine* was again preparing to leave Walvis Bay, bringing a special surf-boat and its expert crew with her. The aircraft made another flight, dropping food and water over the crew of the *Sir Charles Elliott* which had now abandoned their wrecked vessel and had managed to get ashore, and then flying on up the coast and dropping more supplies over the camp. Some of the precious water was lost ; but a few gallons landed safely.

There were now three aircraft at Walvis Bay, and it was decided that one should continue the routine flights with supplies for the castaways ; a second should search for the missing convoy coming overland ; and the third should try a risky landing at a place called Rocky Point to pick up the crew of the tug *Sir Charles Elliott*. All three planes set off early next morning, and the convoy was at last sighted, after being lost for nearly a week during which they had experienced terrible going with the vehicles frequently bogged down in soft sand and tracks having to be cut through virgin bush. At about 5.0 p.m. on December 8th, the convoy moved on in an attempt to reach the camp. They got within 45 miles when fog came down as thick as a blanket and they were forced to camp for the night. However, good work was done that day, for two aircraft managed to save the crew of the tug and fly them back to civilization.

On December 9th the *Nerine* arrived off the camp and anchored. The weather had improved, for the wind had dropped and swell and surf had subsided. The minesweeper hoisted out the surf-boat and lowered one of her lifeboats, and the crews were able to board the stranded *Dunedin Star* on the lee side. The idea was to get a rope ashore, so they lowered one of the big ship's lifeboats and moored her 150 yards from the beach, and also provided a hawser with lifebelts at intervals to keep it afloat. Then they tried firing a thin line ashore by rocket ; but it fell short. They tried again without result. Then a young naval rating from the *Nerine* who was a strong swimmer volunteered to swim ashore with a line. After a severe struggle and no small risk he managed it, and the people ashore tailed on to the thin line and hauled the heavier buoyed hawser to the beach. One man of the shore party pulled himself along it hand over hand and was dragged into the anchored lifeboat. It was a precarious undertaking in the surf ; but during the afternoon 14 more men reached the lifeboat by way of this improvised water-bridge.

It was now the turn of the women and children. With a line out astern to the lifeboat the surf-boat came slowly in towards the beach, which it reached in safety. With eight women and three babies in it besides the crew the surf-boat started to haul off. It rode over one particularly heavy breaker which half-filled the boat with water, drenched everyone on board and gave the passengers a severe fright. It reached the lifeboat and drew alongside. Then, just as the passengers were about to disembark, another huge breaker came roaring down from seaward, capsized the surf-boat, and flung all its occupants into the water. Two of the women and two babies were dragged into the lifeboat. All the rest of the surf-boat's crew and passengers were washed away. They survived by what seems a miracle, and reached the beach half-drowned and utterly exhausted after their ordeal. The surf-boat was washed up after them, shattered and useless for any further operations. At 8.0 p.m. the two lifeboats reached the *Nerine* after an absence of 10 hours, and 19 of the castaways were given hot food and drink and bedded down as comfortably as possible in a small ship with very limited accommodation. That day, December 9th, an aircraft had again been over the camp dropping water and provisions, and bringing also the news that the convoy of vehicles should arrive during the night. But it was not to be. Bogged down again in terrible country the convoy had again to camp for the night.

The wind sprang up and the surf increased during the night of December 9th—10th ; but in the morning the indefatigable *Nerine* sent a boat to the wreck to get bedding, clothing, crockery and what baggage could be found for her rescued people. The surf diminished during the afternoon, so they took the lifeboat back to her moorings of the day before, and again rigged the lifeline to the beach. Eleven more men, including two from the *Nerine* who had landed the day before, pulled themselves to safety. That evening, the *Nerine* sailed for Walvis Bay to land the 26 people she had rescued.

Meanwhile the convoy coming overland was in trouble, and spare springs for the vehicles, with large tarpaulins to enable them to claw out of the soft sand when buried almost to the axles, had to be dropped by aircraft. Getting clear of the salt-pans the trucks crept on. The situation in the camp was easier. Four men had gone off to the *Dunedin Star* in the rubber dinghy and had returned with all the food they could find. They also cut loose two of the life-saving rafts from the wreck in the hope they would drift ashore complete with their water and emergency rations. It was a good idea ; but the rafts just drifted away and were no more seen. Abandoning the rubber dinghy, which was not a very satisfactory sort of craft for use in the surf, they filled a lifeboat with more food and came safely ashore by way of the buoyed lifeline.

By December 12th an aircraft reported that a second convoy of vehicles was about 40 miles behind the first. The first, meanwhile, after much heavy going and using the tarpaulins to reach solid ground, had arrived within six miles of the wreck. No further progress could be made that day ; but at 5.0 p.m. two men from the convoy who had gone on foot reached the castaways. Great was the rejoicing when they arrived. The next day one truck was driven through to the camp and came back with all the provisions and water, which would be needed for the return journey. All the shipwrecked men who were strong enough walked through the six miles of loose sand to where the vehicles were parked. A second truck brought away the women, one small child, and the men who had not been able to make their own way, and by that evening the personnel in the convoy numbered 63 people, rescuers and rescued. The next day, December 14th, the convoy set off for Rocky Point to the southward, whence it was intended to fly the rescued people back to Walvis Bay.

The vehicles had an execrable journey over very bad ground, and part of the time in torrential rain. But they made it in two days, and on December 16th an aeroplane took off with 14 people, including six women and the baby, and landed them safely at Walvis Bay a few minutes after noon. One of the women was pregnant, and it was feared her child would be born in the air, a prospect the doctor did not relish with no instruments or facilities of any sort. As it was the child was born next morning. The aircraft refuelled and returned to Rocky Point, where it landed safely and took off with all the remaining passengers except one, who volunteered to return with the convoy, and six of the *Dunedin Star's* crew in most urgent need of medical attention. They, too, were landed at Walvis Bay.

At 1.0 p.m. on December 24th, 11 trucks comprising the land convoy rolled into Windhoek, the capital of South West Africa. The trip home was abominable ; but with their arrival the last of the passengers and crew of the *Dunedin Star* had been brought home to civilization. Faced with appalling difficulties, the devoted men in those vehicles had accomplished a round trip of 1,500 miles and had won through by their own dogged persistence and refusal to admit defeat.

There, properly, the story should end ; but there still remained Naude's bomber, which had been bogged down in the sand since December 3rd. It was worth £30,000, and must be recovered. Two thousand yards of wire netting had been sent up by rail from Capetown to make a runway over the loose sand. There was also much on board the *Dunedin Star* that was worth salving, and on December 17th, the minesweeper *Crassula* had sailed from Walvis Bay with the salvage party and all its gear. Captain Naude, the pilot of the aircraft and his crew of two, were on board also.

They arrived on December 19th, and the salvage party took up their quarters on board the *Dunedin Star*. The ship was filled with munitions of war which could not be recovered in the very exposed position and with the meagre appliances available. On New Year's Day, 1943, a great storm arose with a very heavy swell and surf which threatened to break the *Dunedin Star's* back. At noon on January 3rd, during a lull in the weather, it was considered advisable to remove the salvage party back to the *Crassula*. They had saved 4,000 bags of mail for the troops in the Middle East and 300 tons of cargo, a remarkable achievement considering the immense difficulties.

The *Crassula* returned to Walvis Bay, where the salvage party, with Naude and his men, were landed after a terrible passage. The latter were sent on to Windhoek by rail, to join an expedition which left there on January 17th. It consisted of eight trucks in all, with a caterpillar tractor mounted on one, and a total complement of 27 men, with Naude in command. I need hardly go into details ; but they reached the bogged aeroplane after many adventures on January 26th. The 'plane was easily pulled out of the sand and the runway laid, and after three days hard work on the engine and controls it was pronounced ready to fly. At about 1.0 p.m. on January 29th Naude, with his two mechanics on board, took off and shaped course for Walvis Bay.

At 1.45, when flying at 300 feet somewhere near Rocky Point, thick smoke started to pour out of the starboard engine, which seized up. Unable to turn to land on the ridge whence the castaways had taken off by air, Naude decided to land in the shallow water between the sand-dunes and the surf. Before he could do this, however, the aircraft nose-dived into the surf about 200 yards from the shore. How her crew survived was a miracle ; but survive they did, though all were badly hurt. The aeroplane itself was a wreck, smashed into three pieces, the wings crumpled and bent with great holes where the engines had fallen out. The tail-planes and rudders had gone, and so had the pilot's cabin and the observer's compartment in the nose.

How those three half-stunned, bruised and bleeding men ever got ashore one cannot imagine ; but after an interminable 45 minutes the floating remains of the aircraft drifted on to a rock about 75 yards from the beach, and the two mechanics, who could just stand, somehow managed to get the more badly-injured Naude to the shore. They were able, too, to save a gallon tin of water and some emergency rations.

They had reached dry land in safety; but even so they were in a most serious fix. The aeroplane's wireless had been out of action, so Naude had not been able to tell anyone they were airborne, which meant they would not be missed. Moreover, the convoy they had just left had no radio link with the outside world, so they would not report the aircraft's departure. The convoy's last link with civilization had been 11 days before, and it would not reach that place on its return journey for at least a week.

Naude sent Rudman, the least injured of his men, on to try to intercept the convoy on its return journey, while he and the third man followed in the same direction. It was agonizing to walk; but for two days they staggered on, carrying their diminishing water and emergency rations under the broiling sun by day as they trudged through the sand, chilled by the wind and heavy dew when they camped at night. They had no blankets, no covering of any kind.

On the afternoon of January 31st, they reached the dry bed of the river near which the convoy must turn inland if it came that way. There, waiting for them was Rudman, who had arrived the night before. He had seen no signs of the convoy, and no fresh tracks so it evidently had not passed. To guard against any possibility of missing the convoy if it went on down the coast instead of striking inland, Rudman was sent down to the river mouth.

By some stroke of luck the convoy had not started on its return journey until January 30th, the day after the aeroplane had left. It was on February 1st, when the vehicles were approaching the mouth of the dried-up river, that they suddenly saw the solitary figure of a man standing on a sand-dune some distance ahead. It was Rudman, who told them of the wrecked plane and of his two companions further inland.

So, by the mercy of Providence, Naude and his two men were saved from certain death, and our story is ended.

CHAPTER XIII

I

CALIFORNIA STAR
March 4th, 1943

THE month of March, 1943, saw the crisis of the battle in the North Atlantic and the peak of the submarine effort. There were more than 100 U-boats at sea and their increasing density made evasive routeing largely nugatory. Such was the strength against us that no area from the Indian Ocean to the Arctic was immune against submarine attack. Large packs of U-boats were operating against the convoys in the North Atlantic, and in March in all areas the Allies lost 108 ships of 627,000 tons through their attacks. The total of ships destroyed was not so high as in the previous May, June or November ; but it was disquieting that the great bulk of the losses occurred in the North Atlantic ; while 85 of the ships sunk were either in convoy or stragglers. The wild weather was partly responsible. The hard-worked escort vessels were small ships, and many were absent from their groups making good the damage sustained in a succession of bitter winter gales.

On the evening of March 4th the 8,300 ton motor-vessel *California Star*, Captain S. Foulkes, on her way from the Panama Canal to Liverpool with a full cargo of refrigerated food and general goods from Australia and New Zealand, was in mid-Atlantic about 380 miles north-west of the island of Flores, in the Azores. Her weather was good ; fine and clear with fair visibility and a slight breeze and swell from the southward. The ship carried four passengers and a crew of 70 officers and men.

At about 7.30 p.m., after dark, when the Chief and Second Officers, Mr. J. Davis and Mr. Cameron Stewart, with a passenger from Panama who had volunteered to keep watch as an extra lookout, the *California Star* was torpedoed twice almost simultaneously on the starboard side of Number 3 hatch. With the crash and shock of the double explosion the engines instantly stopped and all the lights went out. Both the boats on the starboard side were shattered by the blast and the columns of water.

An S.O.S. went out by wireless as soon as the ship was struck, and as soon as Captain Foulkes arrived on the bridge he told the Chief Officer to go forward to clear the rafts ready for letting go. The Second and Third Officers had already gone to the two boats on the port side that remained. While on his way to the wireless room the Captain told the Chief Engineer, Mr. Kilpatrick, that the ship was doomed. He and his men must abandon ship.

The First Wireless Operator, Mr. Robert Stewart, had received no acknowledgment of his S.O.S., so after telling him to continue transmitting the Captain went to the boat-deck. From there he could see that Number 4 lifeboat had been lowered and was leaving the ship's side, so he took charge of the lowering of lifeboat Number 2. When this boat was about three-quarters of the way down a third torpedo struck and exploded immediately beneath it, blowing it to pieces and killing all the occupants. The Captain was blown off his feet, and on recovering looked over the side and could only see the after end of the lifeboat hanging from the davit. After helping several wounded or dazed men Captain Foulkes went aft on the port side, where he saw the Third Officer, Mr. Rackham, getting away the rafts, and then went back to the wireless room. The Operator had sent out nine messages, apparently without any reply, so the Captain told him to leave his instruments and accompany him forward to the rafts.

By this time the *California Star* was sinking by the bows. The water was already breaking through the wash-ports on the fore well-deck. The Captain told Stewart to jump for it ; but instead of that he went aft. As there was nothing more that Captain Foulkes could do, he dived overboard from the starboard side and swam to a small light he could see bobbing about in the water. It was attached to a raft, where he found the Chief Officer, the Third Wireless Operator and two gunners. As he was hauled on board the ship was struck on the port side by a fourth torpedo, and a few minutes later sank by the head. She had lasted about 30 minutes from the time of the first torpedo exploding.

Soon afterwards they saw a larger raft and transferred to it, making fast the one they had left. It was now, for the first time, that they saw the U-boat on the surface coming slowly in their direction. The Captain and Chief Officer took off their uniform jackets, and all of them hid in the bottom of the raft under the screen. The submarine passed quite close ; but the Germans evidently thought the raft was empty, and the U-boat disappeared in the darkness ahead.

After some little time the Captain heard a voice calling ; but not being sure who it was did not reply. Then the voice called, " Brown here. Who's that ? " The Captain then saw it was the lifeboat, so gave instructions to Brown, who was the Ship's Writer, and the senior rating in the boat, to keep in touch through the night. It was not until later that Captain Foulkes discovered that the Second Officer, Mr. Cameron Stewart, who had originally been in charge of the boat, had been taken on board the U-boat as a prisoner of war.

When daylight arrived the lifeboat approached the raft and the Captain discussed the situation with the Chief Officer and others. The lifeboat already contained 23 people. It was unsafe for her to be overcrowded. So it was decided that Captain Foulkes should take charge of the boat and sail her to Flores, 380 miles away. From there, or earlier if he had the luck to meet a ship on the way, he would send help back to those left drifting on the rafts. Before he left the rafts were collected together, and the ship's surgeon, Dr. Erik Pedersen went over to another raft to do all he could for a badly injured man whose case was hopeless. What blankets and food and water could be spared were transferred from the lifeboat to the rafts that wanted them.

The boat, with 24 people on board, sailed off to the south-eastward. We know nothing of the circumstances of the voyage, which took 11 days before she landed at a village in the island of Flores, one boy dying on the way and being buried at sea the day before arrival. Captain Foulkes gave the naval and other authorities the position of the rafts and their probable drift. A vessel was sent to search for them ; but they were never seen again.

In this distressing calamity of a sort that so often happens in a merciless war, 51 people of the 74 originally on board the *California Star* lost their lives.

Nine months later, in the London Gazette of December 7th,

1943, the ship's surgeon, Doctor Erik Pedersen, and the senior radio officer, Mr. Robert Stewart, were posthumously commended. Able Seaman James McMillan, who was specially mentioned by Captain Foulkes as having given the greatest assistance in sailing the boat, was awarded the British Empire Medal.

2

EMPIRE LAKELAND
March 11th, 1943

The loss of the *Empire Lakeland*, Captain F. Gudgin, a 7,000 ton steamer which was not one of the regular vessels of the Blue Star Line but was managed by the Company and on charter to the Admiralty, was another of those mysteries of the war. On February 23rd, 1943, she sailed from New York with a convoy for the United Kingdom carrying a full cargo and a crew of 65. The convoy had fierce weather, with strong westerly gales, a heavy sea and bitter snow squalls, and the *Empire Lakeland*, with another ship, became stragglers. The convoy was fiercely and persistently attacked by U-boats on its passage across the North Atlantic, and the *Empire Lakeland*, with the other vessel the *Empire Impala*, were torpedoed and sunk in about 58°N. 15°W., somewhere near Rockall, on March 11th. Like the *Almeda Star*, which disappeared in much the same spot in January, 1941, no traces of any boats or wreckage were ever discovered.

Among the lost were the First Wireless Officer, Mr. Philip George Winsor, who had received the M.B.E. and Lloyds War Medal for Bravery at Sea for his fine work when the *Sultan Star* was sunk in February, 1940, and Cadet R. Perry, who was commended for his services in the *Empire Star* when that ship was bombed and damaged by Japanese aircraft near Singapore in February, 1942.

3

CANADIAN STAR
March 18th, 1943

The *Canadian Star* has already been mentioned in this narrative on the occasion when, in July, 1941, under the command of Captain C. J. W. Jones, she fought a spirited engagement

135

with a U-boat on the surface at night and escaped after being several times hit. By March, 1943, Captain Jones had been relieved by Captain Robert David Miller, though Mr. P. H. Hunt was still in the ship as Chief Officer and Mr. E. G. Buckwell as Chief Engineer.

On March 8th, carrying 22 passengers and a crew of 69, with a refrigerated and general cargo of about 8,000 tons, the *Canadian Star* sailed from New York for the United Kingdom as one of a convoy of 42 ships. For the first four days, steaming north-eastward, they had fine weather. Reaching a position off the Newfoundland Banks, the convoy turned northward, and on March 12th swung eastward for the passage home. The weather had started to deteriorate, and the forecasts indicated a heavy blow from the north-westward.

By the morning of March 16th, the convoy was almost in mid-Atlantic, nearing that fatal gap some 600 miles south-east of Greenland where it was difficult for aircraft to operate from either side of the ocean and where the U-boats were still hunting in packs. The highest surface speed of the submarines was 18 knots, faster than most of the escorts. Shadowing the convoys at extreme range during daylight, they closed in at dusk. Flooded down with little more than their conning-towers showing they were extremely difficult to spot, particularly as their attacks usually came from the side of the darkest horizon. If necessary they could always dive ; but creeping up at slowly astern of one of the escorts to avoid being discovered by their wash, U-boats would fire their bow torpedoes at selected ships in the convoy and then turn to escape at full speed. If unmolested, torpedo-tubes would be reloaded and another attack made the same night. Convoys might be dogged and attacked at intervals over periods of three and four days on end.

During daylight on the 16th U-boats were in contact with the convoy of which the *Canadian Star* formed a part. The first attacks came when two ships were torpedoed at about 10.0 p.m. At 3.0 a.m. on the 17th more ships were torpedoed, and the convoy made the usual emergency turn away. But the submarines were present in a thick concentration, for at 9.30 a.m. two more ships were hit in quick succession, the first sinking in less than two minutes and the other settling fast as she fell astern and disappeared from the view of those in the *Canadian Star*. How many ships of that convoy were actually torpedoed and sunk on March 16th—17th, I have no means of knowing. In the official Admiralty return of British merchant vessels lost during the war, however, I note that eight British ships—exclusive of any Allied vessels, which the return does not include—are listed as having been sunk in this relatively small area on March 17th. To those in charge of the convoy, no less than to those who were responsible for the organization, this loss was sufficiently perturbing.

The convoy escorts, meanwhile, were counter-attacking by all the means in their power, though here again the Escort Commanders were in their usual predicament. The U-boats were obviously present in force. Was it the duty of the escort vessels to concentrate their efforts on protecting the ships of the convoy that remained ; to stand by and rescue the lives from the ships in distress and sinking ; or to go all out on a counter-offensive against the U-boats ?

It would be presumptuous for anyone not actually on the spot and knowing all the circumstances to venture any opinion as to what ought to be done by the escorts at any given moment. But this much can be said. Because of the heavy strain on our resources in many widely-scattered areas, there were insufficient escort vessels to do all three jobs at once.

To add to their difficulties and perplexities, the weather was steadily becoming worse. By the evening of the 17th it was blowing a roaring gale from the north-west, with a high, tumbling, steep sea and heavy swell with occasional heavy squalls of sleet and hail. The *Canadian Star* was a ship of more than 8,000 gross tons. Steaming at the revolutions for 10 knots she was making good no more than between six and seven. If this was the case in a big ship, the conditions in the much smaller destroyers and corvettes must have been indescribable.

The convoy steamed on, and at 2.38 p.m. on March 18th the ship ahead of the *Canadian Star* was suddenly torpedoed on the port side. Alarm bells were rung, and Mr. Keyworth, the Third Officer, who was on watch, shouted " Hard 'a starboard ! Everyone off the port side of the deck ! " At much the same moment the periscope of a U-boat was sighted about 100 feet away on the port beam. The ship started to swing to starboard ; but it was too late to do any more. Almost immediately the ship was hit simultaneously by two torpedoes on the port side, one in the engine-room and the other in Number 5 hold.

The engines stopped at once, one torpedo actually striking

one of the cylinders of the main engines. Two boats, which were swung out, were blown into fragments.. The hatches were blasted off Number 5 hold and the ship was partially wrecked amidships, half the chartroom being demolished and blown upwards on to the " monkey island " overhead. The ship settled rapidly by the stern, and the after deck was soon awash with the great seas breaking and surging over it. Orders were given to abandon ship. There was nothing else to be done.

Mr. Hunt, the Chief Officer, took charge of the passengers and crew, and as Captain Miller did not survive, here seems the appropriate place to quote what Hunt afterwards said of him :

" I should like to mention the calm gallantry of Captain D. R. Miller, who did everything possible for the safety and welfare of his passengers and crew. His only concern was to see that everyone abandoned ship successfully, without the slightest consideration for his own safety. He was an exceptionally fine seaman, and his quiet, cool behaviour set a magnificent example to all."

The stricken *Canadian Star* was sinking fast. The signal of distress had already been sent off by wireless. Mr. Hunt directed passengers and crew to the starboard side of the boat-deck, where Numbers 1 and 3 lifeboats were turned out and ready for lowering. While Number 3 was being lowered with people in it, the after fall unfortunately took charge and the boat descended with a run. Hung by the bows three passengers were tipped out and lost. It was eventually lowered with 12 people in it, but capsized in the raging sea.

After this sad mishap Mr. Hunt, to quote his own report :

" Went once again to the after deck to make sure the ship was sinking before launching Number One boat, as I considered the chances of a successful launching to be small. I found the after deck under water, with the port rafts smashed away by the high seas. Number One boat was then launched with as many people as the davits would support, and orders were given by the Captain to man and launch the starboard rafts. All four starboard rafts were successfully launched and saved many lives, while Number Three boat was successfully righted and manned with the Third Officer in charge."

All the survivors were clear of the ship by 2.55, Captain Miller having last been seen on the boat deck. The ship finally sank stern first at 3.10, her bows rearing up and remaining vertical for nearly five minutes before they plunged under.

There were 26 people in Number 1 boat. It was numbingly cold, and everyone, particularly those on the rafts, suffered terribly from exposure. As Hunt writes :

" Practically the whole crew were accommodated in the two boats and the rafts, and the large loss of life was due to the weather. Number One boat picked up all they could from the water until it was crowded. Number Three boat capsized twice and many were lost there. The rafts that were properly manned stood up to the weather, while the ones with few people in them were capsized by the tops of the waves, causing loss of life."

Within two hours all the visible living survivors were picked up by the corvettes H.M.S.'s *Anemone* and *Pennywort*. Rolling, pitching and plunging dizzily these two little ships went about the work of rescue. It required the greatest nicety of judgment and good seamanship. One of the corvettes went alongside the waterlogged Number 3 boat, Keyworth's, in which only five or six people remained, all the others having been washed away. As a result of their experiences one of the lady passengers, and Mr. E. G. Buckwell, the *Canadian Star's* Chief Engineer, died soon after being rescued. Nothing more could be done. After rescuing all the survivors they could find the *Anemone* and *Pennywort* steamed on at their best speed to rejoin the convoy ahead. By this time it was dark. They encountered U-boats on the way, running in to attack with guns and depth-charges. More attacks were made on the convoy during the night of March 18th—19th, though so far as my records show no further ships were sunk. For the last part of the voyage the sorely-tried escorts were reinforced by two American destroyers from Iceland, while further east they had the additional protection of aircraft.

Mr. Hunt was on board the *Anemone*, which carried in all 154 survivors from various ships. How they fared in vile weather in the limited accommodation of a small corvette we are not told; but at 2.30 p.m. on March 22nd they were landed at Gourock with thankfulness in their hearts. Of the total of 91 people in the *Canadian Star* 32 had perished.

The experiences of this convoy and of the *Canadian Star* were by no means exceptional. They were typical of what was happening all over the North Atlantic at this particular period of the U-boat war, a struggle in which the seamen of the Royal and the Merchant Navies, working together, were pitting their strength, their resource and, above all, their courage, against the craftiest and most deadly of opponents. It was a fight which knew no mercy or quarter, a struggle which that past-master of the apt phrase, Mr. Winston Churchill, described as a war " of groping and drowning, of ambuscade and stratagem, of science and seamanship."

It is pleasing to know that in the official London Gazette of

August 31st, 1943, the gallant Captain Robert David Miller of the *Canadian Star*, was posthumously commended. (This, the equivalent of a " mention in despatches," is the only official recognition, apart from the Victoria Cross or the George Cross, that can be awarded to a dead person for gallantry in death).

In the same Gazette, Mr. Percival Herbert Hunt and Mr. Reginald Herbert Keyworth, the Chief and the Third Officers, were both awarded the M.B.E. After describing how the *Canadian Star* was torpedoed and sunk, the citation continues :

" On abandonment, the Third Officer took charge of one of the boats, and, under his direction, it was twice righted after it had been capsized by the heavy seas. Eventually six survivors in this boat were picked up and saved. But for Mr. Keyworth's courage, determination and leadership, these lives would probably have been lost.

The Chief Officer set an outstanding example by his courage and coolness. He assisted in getting away the boats in the short space of time available, and, by his organization and efficiency, ensured the safety of many lives."

4

CELTIC STAR
March 29th, 1943

On March 28th, 1943, the 5,600 ton steamer *Celtic Star* sailed independently from Freetown for Montevideo and Buenos Ayres. She carried a crew of 64 and two passengers, and was commanded by Captain James Hunter Andrew Mackie, M.B.E., who had been Chief Officer of the *Sydney Star* during her voyage to Malta with a convoy in August, 1941.

The weather was good, and at about 10 o'clock on the night of the 29th the ship was about 360 miles south-west of Freetown zig-zagging on her course. It was very dark with good visibility, a gentle north-easterly breeze, and a slight sea.

Ten minutes later the ship was suddenly torpedoed on the starboard side abreast of Number 2A hold, a vital spot. Having checked the position on the chart Captain Mackie told his senior wireless officer, Mr. J. Murphy, to send out the usual radio distress signal, which was done at once.

As it was clear that the ship was sinking the Captain gave orders for her to be abandoned. The engines were stopped and he rang down " Finished with engines," which was the signal for those below to abandon ship. At 10.12 p.m. the ship was hit by a second torpedo on the starboard side abreast of Number 3 hold. Two of the lifeboats were completely wrecked by the successive explosions.

The other two boats were safely manned and lowered. Remaining on board there were now about 25 men, so splitting them up into groups the Captain ordered them to launch the forward and after life-saving rafts. He personally went forward and superintended the launching of the forward rafts and told the men to get into the water after them. Returning to the bridge the Captain was told by the wireless operator, Mr. Murphy, that the S.O.S. had gone out four times. So, as the Captain wrote in his report : " I instructed him to come with me and abandon the ship, for we could do no more. We met the Third Engineer (Mr. J. Nuttall) on the lower bridge, so I said ' We'll launch our small jolly boat and get away.' We were in the act of doing this when I shouted ' Jump for your lives ! She's sinking fast ! ' and after seeing them slip overboard I followed. In less than 30 seconds I heard a muffled explosion, presumably boilers bursting. Fortunately the vessel still had a little headway, for I was taken down a short distance with the suction."

In the complete darkness and strong current several men were holding on to wreckage in the water waiting to be picked up by the boats. Captain Mackie himself was about 45 minutes swimming amongst the litter of flotsam and thick scum of oil fuel before he was picked up by the boat in charge of the Fourth Officer, Mr. W. K. Thomas. Altogether, 17 people were rescued from the water by this boat and eight others by the boat in which was the Chief Officer, Mr. W. Tulip.

" I distinctly heard the diesel engines of the submarine," Captain Mackie wrote of the period that followed. " I fully expected she would be searching for me. She kept morse signalling calling up letter A's, so I ordered the men to row hard and steered in an opposite direction. I repeated this manœuvre four times and so managed to elude her. My Chief Officer was not so fortunate, for he was sighted by the submarine and ordered to go alongside. They first enquired for the Captain and were told I had gone down with the ship, as they really thought. They next asked the ship's name and number of crew carried. Following this they said ' Any officers in the boat ? ' and receiving no reply they grabbed the nearest man, saying ' You'll do.' This man proved to be J. Pattison A.B. and he is to be commended for leaving silently. The U-boat next enquired 'Do you want anything?' Some asked for cigarettes, and they were handed Italian cigarettes and Argentine matches. Just before the submarine left they were at pains to emphasize 'Don't forget Italiano submarine sink your ship!'"

When daylight came hours later the Captain's boat rowed over to the Chief Officer's and they called a muster. They found that three men were missing; but a little later, hearing faint cries, they rowed over and picked up a fireman who had been clinging to wreckage all through the night. After a stimulant he was none the worse for his experience.

As the distress signal with the ship's position had gone out, the Captain decided to remain on the spot for 24 hours, so they rowed over to the abandoned rafts and removed all the fresh water and provisions, a wise precaution. This done Captain Mackie made a little speech to his men, telling them, in so many words, that they had absolutely nothing to worry about. "We've enough food and water for five weeks," he added. "If we have to row, because there's no wind, we can make the nearest land in seven or eight days."

The wireless masts were rigged and the wireless officer sent out the position several times by the lifeboat transmitter. The weather remained fine, and that night—March 30th—31st—the boats remained together. At daylight they again used the lifeboat's radio, but had no reply. Two unidentified aircraft were in sight at this time; but showed no signs of having noticed the boats.

"Having dismantled wireless masts, and rigged masts and sails," Captain Mackie's report continues, "I now informed my Chief Officer that we would part company and make for the nearest land, Freetown, which I estimated was 360 miles distant and to steer between north-east and east-north-east and wished them good luck. We rowed with sails set until noon, when I had water and rations distributed."

Their troubles were soon over, for at 12.45 both boats were sighted by a Sunderland flying-boat which circled overhead, and at about 5.0 p.m. the Captain sighted a small vessel, H.M.S. *Wastwater*, which picked up the crews of both boats before dark. Before getting alongside their rescuer Captain Mackie made another little speech to his men. "Now remember," he said, "we've all had a very easy time with little or no hardship, so when you get on board this ship I want none of you to grumble or complain, but just uphold the honour of the Merchant Navy to which you belong." The men applauded and cheered him.

In the sinking of the *Celtic Star* two men were lost, and another, as already described, was made a prisoner of war by the submarine. The survivors reached Freetown on April 2nd, whence most of them were repatriated to England.

" Before concluding my report," Captain Mackie wrote, " I would mention that all the members of my crew behaved admirably and carried out all my orders without the slightest panic or confusion. I wish to make special mention and recommendation of my Senior Radio Officer, Mr. J. Murphy, for standing by me until the very last minute, and the Third Engineer, Mr. J. Nuttall, who remained below to stop the engines under great difficulty. Their courage and devotion to duty was outstanding, especially as the vessel foundered in 12 minutes."

In the London Gazette of August 31st, 1943, the announcement was made that Captain James Hunter Andrew Mackie, M.B.E., had been awarded the O.B.E., and that the Third Engineer, Mr. James Nuttall, had been given the M.B.E. The Senior Radio Officer, John Murphy, was commended. After recounting the circumstances in which the *Celtic Star* was torpedoed and sunk, the citation continued :

" The Master acted with courage, coolness and resource throughout. It was due to his excellent organization and leadership that in the difficult and dangerous circumstances the ship was successfully abandoned. The Third Engineer Officer, although not on watch when the ship was hit, went below and, at great personal risk from escaping fumes, succeeded in stopping the engines. This materially assisted the successful launching of the boats and rafts. In order to stop the engines Mr. Nuttall had to obtain suitable tools from the refrigerator space while the ship was sinking. He completed his task and reached the deck just in time to jump clear as the ship sank."

5

MELBOURNE STAR
April 2nd, 1943

On March 22nd, 1943, the *Melbourne Star* sailed from Liverpool on her way to Sydney through the Panama Canal. She carried a crew of 86 with 31 passengers, and was commanded by Captain James Bennett Hall, whose name will be remembered as having been in command of the *Andalucia Star* when that vessel was sunk by an U-boat on October 6th, 1942. Among those on board the *Melbourne Star* who had been in her during her historic voyage to Malta in August, 1942, were the Chief Officer, Mr. L. Parsons ; Mr. H. Blandford, the Chief Engineer; Mr. C. W. Almond, the Chief Refrigerating Engineer ; Mr. W. E. Richards, the Second Officer, and Mr. J. Cook, the Boatswain.

The ship carried a heavy cargo of torpedoes, ammunition and other munitions of war, and once clear of the most dangerous submarine area sailed unescorted.

We know few of the details of her loss, except that at about 3.0 a.m. on April 2nd, when 480 miles south-east of Bermuda in the bad weather that was raging all over the North Atlantic, she was struck by two torpedoes almost simultaneously. The double explosion detonated portions of her dangerous cargo, for three-quarters of the vessel were destroyed in a flash. The explosions were so sudden and devastating that neither passengers nor crew could muster at their boat stations, even if any boats had been left intact. Practically the entire complement perished simultaneously, and the shattered remains of the ship went to the bottom in less than two minutes. As she foundered several of the life-saving rafts floated free to which a few of the survivors managed to scramble. Their plight was made even worse by the heavy sea and low visibility, and when the dawn came only 11 people were left alive on the rafts.

At daylight the U-boat approached the two rafts in turn and her commander questioned the occupants as to the name of the ship and the nature of her cargo. Then they were left to their own resources, and the rafts drifted apart. There had been no chance to send off an S.O.S., and the first news of the *Melbourne Star* loss came through the usual boastful German broadcast.

One of the rafts was never seen or heard of again. The other, which contained four men named W. Best, W. Burns, R. Nunn, and L. White, had on board eight tins of biscuits, some tins of chocolate, malted milk tablets, pemmican, 22 gallons of water and a two gallon tin of massage oil for use against exposure. By the mercy of Providence the weather remained stormy for only three days, after which it became calm and they just drifted at the mercy of the breeze and current. Improvising fishing lines they caught about 50 fish, which, eaten raw, probably saved their lives. The special oil was most valuable.

Every morning when daylight came they gazed round the heaving horizon, hoping for the sight of a ship or perhaps a feather of smoke moving in their direction. Each morning they were disappointed. The great ocean remained barren, shining like burnished steel in the glare of the sun. The days passed in dreadful monotony and anxiety. Many times they gave themselves up for lost, wondering, perhaps, what would happen when their water was exhausted.

It was on May 9th, 38 days after the *Melbourne Star* had been sunk, that they were sighted by an American flying boat which came down on the water and taxied alongside. After a flight of two and a half hours they were landed at Bermuda. They were all covered in salt water ulcers and had to have medical attention ; but considering the length of time they had been adrift were in unusually good condition.

In the London Gazette of August 15th, 1944, 16 months after their rescue, it was announced that William Best, Greaser ; William Joseph Burns, Greaser ; Ronald Nunn, Ordinary Seaman ; and Leonard White, Able Seaman, had all been awarded the British Empire Medal for " outstanding qualities of courage, fortitude and endurance which enabled them to survive the hardships and perils of the long and hazardous ordeal on the raft."

Nunn did not survive to receive his award. He lost his life by enemy action in S.S. *Dungrange* when that vessel was torpedoed and sunk by an E boat off St. Catherine's Point, Isle of Wight, on June 10th, 1944.

6

By the end of March, 1943, the strength of the U-boat effort was becoming temporarily exhausted, and the offensive at sea was passing into the hands of the Allies, though this is not to say that the battle of the Atlantic was finally won.

The enemy lost 15 U-boats in March, 16 in April, and 45 in May. Nowhere in the North Atlantic were they immune from attack by long-range aircraft or surface vessels. By the third week in May the tide had definitely turned in our favour. Submarines were being destroyed at a rate which substantially exceeded the output of the German building yards, and by the beginning of June they had virtually been withdrawn from the convoy routes in the North Atlantic. Their spasmodic activity had been diverted to the safer areas off Rio de Janeiro, Freetown and in the Mozambique Channel.

Our losses at sea declined rapidly. Five fine ships of the Blue Star Line had been sunk by U-boats during March and April in the circumstances already described. From the beginning of May until the end of the year the company had no losses at all, though two of their ships were damaged.

On May 2nd, 1943, while steaming with a convoy off West Africa, the *Empire Might*, commanded by Captain S. J. C. Phillips, who had been Master of the *Imperial Star* when that ship was sunk during a voyage to Malta with a convoy in September, 1941, caught fire in the stokehold. Few details are available; but the engines were out of action for the time being and the ship had to be taken in tow by the destroyer *Ashanti*. Later the tow had to be cast off because the destroyer was running short of fuel. In the meanwhile, however, the *Empire Might's* engineers, under the direction of Mr. Richard William Brown, the Chief Engineer, managed to get the engines running and the ship steaming at 12 knots. She proceeded to Dakar for temporary repairs, and then went on to Freetown, where fire again broke out amidst the ammunition.

Throughout the period May 2nd to 14th the situation was difficult and dangerous, and for their fine work in dealing with the fire and saving their ship and the valuable cargo, Captain Samuel John Clement Phillips; the Chief Officer, Mr. Dominic Joseph Stratta; and the Fourth Engineer, Mr. Alfred Douglas Fraser, were all officially commended in the London Gazette dated November 19th, 1943. Mr. Brown, the Chief Engineer of the *Empire Might*, in the London Gazette dated January 3rd, 1945, was awarded the O.B.E. for long and meritorious service in the Merchant Navy.

Another incident of which I have no precise details was when the Blue Star vessel *Empire Highway* at sea off the Portuguese coast with a convoy, was subjected to a high level bombing attack by enemy aircraft on July 7th, 1943. There were no casualties, though the ship was considerably shaken and suffered slight damage through near misses.

CHAPTER XIV

I

ROYAL STAR
April 21st, 1944

EMPIRE JAVELIN
December 28th, 1944

TO continue the overall picture of the submarine war to its conclusion, the beginning of June, 1943, saw the virtual withdrawal of the U-boats from the Atlantic. Some 80 submarines were still at sea ; but their activities were namely concentrated off Rio de Janeiro, off Freetown and in the Mozambique Channel, all outside the normal range of shore-based aircraft.

From time to time U-boats had been seen in the calm weather zone 500-700 miles south-west of the Azores, an area which was assuming even greater importance than usual because it was on the route used by the convoys carrying troops and supplies to North Africa and the Mediterranean for the impending invasion of Sicily. The area could not adequately be protected by shore-based aircraft, and the gap was now filled by escort-carriers of the United States Navy with marked success. In the approaches to the Bay of Biscay, too, as well as between the Faeroes and Iceland, aircraft of Coastal Command of the R.A.F. were harrying the submarines in transit to and from their bases in France, Norway and Germany. Seventeen U-boats were destroyed at sea by the Allies during June, and no fewer than 46 in July. August, 1943, too was a lean month for the enemy, in which for the first time the Allies sank more submarines than the submarines sank merchant ships. Twenty-three U-boats were destroyed for 16 merchant ships of about 86,000 gross tons. In the Bay of Biscay nine U-boats were actually sunk in one week.

It was in September, 1943, that there came a resumption of the attacks upon the convoys in the North Atlantic. The Germans had little choice in the matter, for it was only here that they could interfere with the development of the Allied plans and the build-up of the armies in Britain for the subsequent invasion of the Continent of Europe. The enemy were trying out new tactics and new weapons. These latter were acoustic torpedoes homed on to their targets by the sound of fast-running propellers, and intended primarily for use against the escorts. All U-boats operating against convoys carried three or four of them, the idea being to destroy a fair number of the escorts and then to use ordinary torpedoes for sinking the unprotected merchant ships.

The offensive at sea had definitely passed into our hands ; but the battle against the U-boats was not yet won. They were still operating far afield in the Indian Ocean and the Gulf of Aden, and were endeavouring to pass more and more submarines into the Mediterranean, which had been opened to mercantile traffic soon after the surrender of the Axis armies in Tunisia in May, 1943. In the following September, simultaneously with the landing at Salerno, came Italy's unconditional surrender. But the last two U-boats in the Mediterranean were not finally eliminated until September, 1944, up till which time our merchant ships continued to sail in convoy. This was all the more necessary because ships moving along the North African coast were still liable to attack by German aircraft from northern Italy or the south of France.

2

ROYAL STAR
April 21st, 1944

On the afternoon of April 20th, 1944, the steamship *Royal Star* of 8,000 tons, commanded by Captain Thomas Francis McDonald, sailed from Algiers to join up with a large westbound convoy off that port. The cargo consisted of about 5,300 tons of frozen meat and 350 tons of dehydrated meat for Malta, Taranto and Alexandria. The ship, which had 73 people on board, also carried eight naval torpedoes consigned to Malta.

That evening at about 6 o'clock the *Royal Star* duly joined up with the convoy, which had an American Commodore in charge and an American escort. The great mass of ships steamed on to the westward in formation at $7\frac{1}{2}$ knots, the sea being glassily calm with faint catspaws of breeze ruffling its surface in patches. It was fine and clear, with a slight haze over the horizon.

At 9.0 p.m., off Cape Bengut in the last of the twilight, those in the *Royal Star* heard the sound of aircraft engines. This was soon followed by gunfire and streams of coloured tracer on the port wing of the convoy. A quarter of an hour later a ship in the centre of the convoy blew up with a great flash and thundering report, to send a pile of dark smoke wreathing to the heavens. The attack was being made by a considerable number of low-flying torpedo-bombers, which seemed to be streaming in from all directions at once. Within a few minutes all the *Royal Star's* guns were in action, a long burst from the Oerlikon on the port side of her bridge being seen to go fairly into the fuselage of one aircraft which passed close under her stern. Her starboard guns were concentrating their fire on more aircraft coming in from the south.

At about this time, in the medley of heavy gunfire, two more violent explosions were heard to port and ahead, suggesting that two more ships had been torpedoed. Things were happening in split seconds, and at 9.20 an aircraft roared in on the *Royal Star's* starboard beam at less than masthead height, dropped his torpedo at pointblank range, banked steeply and vanished astern, narrowly escaping the balloon wire. A burst from one of the guns was put into his belly as he banked ; but it was impossible to see the result.

Meanwhile, it was impossible for the torpedo to miss. It struck the *Royal Star* square between the engine-room and stokehold, killing one man and demolishing the bulkhead and oil-fuel settling tank. Number 1 lifeboat, which was turned out, together with its davits, was flung high over the boat-deck and fell in splinters on Number 4 hatch. The boat abaft it, Number 3, was blown clean away and landed in the water astern, its davits being bent almost double by the blast. The stokehold and engine-room filled immediately to sea level, and the deck and superstructure were thickly coated in oil fuel. The whole ship became shrouded in smoke and steam.

Captain McDonald ordered the usual signal to be made by wireless and the after holds to be sounded. Numbers 4 and 5 were found to be making water, and the ship took a slight list to starboard. Inspection showed there was no hope of getting a mat over the hole to keep down the flow of water. However, the weather was fine and the land fairly close, and the Captain had every hope of saving his ship and cargo if a tow could be obtained in time. Meanwhile she lay helpless.

Before long the convoy and escort had passed out of sight and the *Royal Star* was alone. At about 11.0 p.m. an American escort destroyer appeared, but would not come very close. To quote Captain McDonald :

"I signalled him repeatedly ' Confident of salvage. Close me and pass a line,' and later, ' You may close me with safety ' ; but without result. Eventually a Lieutenant and a Pharmacist's Mate boarded, and the latter dressed the injuries of A. Triggs, A.B. I urged on the Lieutenant the strong probability of salvage if his ship would take me in tow without delay. This, he claimed, he was unable to do, but signalled that a tug would be sent out, parted company, and was not seen again."

One can forgive Captain McDonald's natural exasperation ; but in justice to the American it is probable he had other orders. In the best conditions it was unlikely that a small escort vessel of about 1,000 tons displacement could have made anything of a job of towing a ship like the *Royal Star* with a deadweight tonnage of at least 14,000, particularly if the large vessel was without her steering gear. Moreover, the American had probably been sent back to save life, and in the circumstances lives were hardly in danger. The weather was fine, the shore was not far off and a tug had been asked for. Algiers was within 30 miles.

At 1.30 a.m. on the 21st Captain McDonald decided that the convoy was too far away to be endangered by submarines or aircraft if he used full power on his wireless. Accordingly he sent off. " S.O.S.—REQUIRE ASSISTANCE URGENTLY. STRONG PROBABILITY OF SALVAGE. SEND TUGS." This message was repeated at half-hourly intervals, and between the transmissions " homing " signals were made to guide any vessel to the spot, and white rockets were fired. The last signal was made at 2.50 a.m., with the auxiliary batteries nearly run down and the radiation very weak. The last of the rockets had been used. " The position at this time," Captain McDonald wrote, was : " engine-room and stokehold full to sea level ; Number 3 hold, 4 feet of water ; Number 4, 14 feet ; Number 5, 15 feet ; Number 6, 9 feet. After peak full to sea level. Crew's quarters flooding. After freeboard was five feet, and all compartments mentioned above making water rapidly. I then deemed it advisable to send the crew away and gave the order ' Abandon ship,' which was carried out in excellent order, myself remaining on board. The boats remained close to the ship. During this period I saw a steamer stopped and lying low in the water about three miles away on my port beam, and several times throughout the night I attempted to attract her attention by Aldis lamp and pistol shots without success. I presumed her to have been a ship damaged and probably abandoned. She had disappeared at dawn. After the crew abandoned ship I made repeated inspections and found that the vessel was gradually settling."

By 7.30 a.m. H.M. Rescue Tug *Athlete*, Lieutenant Cole, R.N.R., which had come out from Algiers, went alongside. Her hawser was passed across and secured, and towing started at 8.0 a.m. The *Royal Star's* crew, meanwhile had been taken out of their boats by an American destroyer and then transferred to the *Athlete*. Course was shaped for Algiers at a speed of about two knots ; but as soon as towing began the water started to gain fast and it became obvious that the ship would never make port. The coastline in the vicinity is steep to and rocky, and completely unsuitable for beaching. However, the ship was sinking, and at about 10.30 it was decided to steer in for the beach in a last effort to save her. Captain McDonald, apparently, was on board alone.

" At about 10.50," he wrote, " the ship began to settle rapidly and I felt heavy rumblings underfoot and believed Number 516 bulkhead to have gone at this time. At 11.2 the tug ceased towing and cast off. The ship began to stand on end, and at 11.7 she was vertical and I jumped clear at Number 2 hatch as she went under. . . . I was subsequently picked up by H.M. Motor Launch 568, unhurt except for bruises caused by wreckage shooting to the surface. The M.L. proceeded to Algiers, passing *Athlete* on the way. . . . I landed there at 2.30 p.m. followed by the crew at 3 o'clock."

In the London Gazette of August 29th, 1944, it was announced that Captain Thomas Francis McDonald had been awarded the O.B.E. The Chief Engineer, Mr. James William Innes, who had already been awarded the O.B.E. in June, 1943, for long and meritorious service in the Merchant Navy, was commended, as was Archibald Angus MacKinnon, the *Royal Star's* Boatswain. The official citation ran :

" The ship was sailing in a convoy which was attacked by enemy aircraft. She was hit by a torpedo. Considerable damage was caused and the engines put out of action. Despite this, the Master determined to try to save the vessel. The ship could not proceed under her own steam and was taken in tow, but she sank soon after towage commenced. Captain McDonald displayed courage, determination and seamanship of a high order. When the convoy was attacked the ship put up an excellent defence under his command. After the vessel was hit he realized the danger to his crew and ordered the boats away. He remained on board himself, however, in a gallant attempt to save the ship, and did not leave until she sank beneath him."

In addition to the O.B.E. Captain McDonald was also awarded Lloyds War Medal for Bravery at Sea.

3

It was in January, 1944, that Grand Admiral Doenitz, Commander-in-Chief of the German Navy, said at a conference at Stettin : " The enemy has succeeded in gaining the advantage in submarine defence ; but the day will come when I shall offer Churchill a first-rate submarine war. The submarine weapon has not been broken by the set-backs of 1943. On the contrary, it has become stronger. In 1944, which will be a successful but a hard year, we shall smash Britain's supply with a new submarine weapon." It is to be noted that the passage quoted was omitted in all versions of the Grand Admiral's speech broadcast inside Germany.

A month before this, addressing flag officers of the German Navy, Doenitz had referred to the heavy U-boat losses during the summer of 1943, and had then spoken of creating what was virtually a new Navy, far greater and stronger than anything that had gone before. " I alone cannot do this," he had added. " It can only be done by the man who controls European production, Speer, who bears the responsibility, before the Fuehrer and the German people, for having the new vessels ready for us on the appointed day."

The effectiveness of the British " radar " fitted in all surface warships and aircraft, had led to the enemy's development of the " Schnorkel," which permitted the U-boats to remain under water for long periods, and to charge their batteries while submerged. Enemy scientists had already designed the " V.1 " and " V.2 " weapons which later wrought such harm and destruction. What Grand Admiral Doenitz referred to, however, were submarines of an entirely new type. They had a high submerged speed with streamlined hulls, and a very long seagoing endurance.   Pre-fabricated all over German occupied territory in Europe, it was intended that 350 of the new boats should be in operation by April, 1945.

The advent of these new U-boats would have revolutionized submarine warfare.   With greatly improved " Schnorkels " to permit them to remain under water for long periods, they would have been very difficult to detect from the air.   While submerged their speed would have been comparable to the escort vessels, and on the surface they were considerably faster.   They would have been extremely difficult to counter, particularly in bad weather.

The process of assembling these new U-boats was greatly retarded by the intensive Allied bombing of the German factories, ship yards, railways and canals.   Their design, too, was even more complicated than usual, and their teething troubles took a lot of getting over.   Teutonic ingenuity and thoroughness rather defeated their own ends, for picked and experienced officers and men who might have been manning operational U-boats of the older type at sea were battling with the many defects and difficulties of the new boats when they first underwent their trials.   Their mass production that had been envisaged was not possible by the time Germany was forced into unconditional surrender.

By May, 1944, when the enemy realized that invasion was imminent, a few U-boats were operating against the convoys to North Russia, while others were in the Mediterranean, or striving to get there through the Straits of Gibraltar.   Some of the larger submarines, unsuitable for anti-invasion duties, were also operating in the Caribbean or Indian Ocean.   But the bulk of the German 500-ton U-boats were in Norwegian ports, or the much-battered harbour in the Bay of Biscay, preparing to attack our invasion convoys across the Channel.

The landing of the Allied armies in Normandy started on June 6th, 1944, and the English Channel became flooded with an immense volume of shipping of every sort and description, including warships.   There were still more than 70 U-boats in operation, and apart from the larger boats in the Caribbean and Indian Ocean, the Germans still had sufficient submarines to launch heavy mass attacks on the Channel convoys.   In theory they might have saturated the defence and have jeopardized the success of the landings in Normandy.   A few U-boats, using their Schnorkels, did get through the defences towards the end of June and operate in the invasion area; but their efforts did not greatly affect the stream of men and supplies across the Channel.

Because of the success of the anti-submarine war in the North Atlantic, we were able to reduce the number of escort vessels there and use them for the cross-Channel convoys. But the aircraft of Coastal Command, Royal Air Force, really formed the first line of defence by " flooding " the whole area from the south of Ireland to the Biscayan port of Lorient, including the western part of the Channel. On D-day, June 6th, U-boats started to stream out of their Biscay bases, travelling at full speed on the surface in their haste to reach the invasion area. They met the full blast of the Coastal Command aircraft, and in the first four critical days, June 6th-10th, 36 U-boats were sighted by day or by night, 23 were attacked, six were sunk and about the same number badly damaged.

After D—4 the Germans changed their tactics. Submarines using Schnorkel attempted to creep past the patrolling aircraft. Of these seven more were sunk by aircraft and surface forces. In the first six months of 1944 the enemy had lost 122 U-boats through Allied action by sea and air, with many more damaged. Badly mauled, though not yet defeated, they were now risking nothing more than was absolutely necessary.

As early as June 13th Doenitz was advising Hitler that the submarines stationed in the Bay of Biscay were to be withdrawn, because " they risk serious losses in that area while being of no practical value," and that it had to be kept in mind that it might become necessary to recall all submarines to Norway.

This withdrawal, with very heavy losses, began in August, and for the U-boats it was the beginning of the end.

4

EMPIRE JAVELIN
December 28th, 1944

The *Empire Javelin* of 7,200 tons, commanded by Captain John McLean, was the last of the Blue Star ships to be lost in the war. After the Allied landings in Normandy she was one of the vessels engaged in carrying troops and stores across the Channel, and at first light on December 28th, 1944, carrying

1,448 soldiers of the United States Army, she sailed from Southampton for Havre. Another ship was with her ; but the *Empire Javelin* was leading. The pair were escorted by the French frigate *L'Escaramouche*.

The little convoy had been ordered to proceed at its best speed, which was about 12½ knots. They were off the Nab Tower at 11.50 a.m., and at about 2.30 p.m. were some 40 miles to the southward of the Isle of Wight, or roughly in mid-Channel.

10 minutes later there was a heavy explosion under the *Empire Javelin*, which Captain McLean thought was a mine. It was, in fact, the torpedo from a U-boat, which so damaged the ship that the engine-room and Number 4 hold were immediately flooded. One officer and three men of the engine-room staff were killed at once ; but Mr. S. A. Hill, an Assistant Engineer, managed to come up through the escape section of the funnel.

All the troops and crew mustered at their emergency stations, and the wounded were put in the two lifeboats. Captain McLean thought the ship would float for some time ; but considered it advisable that the troops should be removed. To quote the Captain's report :

" A signal was sent to the escort to try and come alongside for wounded only. This signal was then cancelled, the escort saying that she could not come alongside. So the two boats were lowered into the water and with all the known wounded. At 3.0 p.m. another signal was sent to the escort insisting that she come alongside. This signal was acknowledged by ' L'Escaramouche.' She came alongside, and I gave orders to abandon ship. While she was alongside a man who had been trapped in Number Four hatch was released by burning a ventilator."

All the troops and all the crew except six officers and three men, who elected to remain behind with the Captain, were safely transferred to the French frigate, which then lay off and transferred them to two L.S.T's—Landing Ships, Tank— which had arrived on the scene. In the meantime a signal had been sent off asking for tugs.

The *Empire Javelin* lay waiting and helpless, until, in the dark of the evening at 5.15, there was another very heavy explosion in Number 5 hold. The U-boat had fired a second torpedo, though why she had delayed for so long it is impossible to say.

The ship was practically blown to pieces and sunk in about a minute. All those on board took to the water, with the exception of the Third Officer, David Robinson, who had gone to his cabin just before the explosion took place. Three Able Seamen, Douglas William Southgate ; Charles James Percy Shaw ; and William Howard Vincent, were seen swimming away from the ship as she went under. Of these three only Vincent survived.

Captain McLean, with five others, managed to reach a raft, and were eventually picked up by a boat from *L'Escaramouche*. In all seven people were lost when the *Empire Javelin* was torpedoed and when she finally went to the bottom.

In the London Gazette of August 14th, 1945, the names of the following were noted as having been commended for their services when the *Empire Javelin* was sunk :

> Captain John McLean.
> Chief Officer Joseph Alec Cucksey.
> Third Officer David Robinson (deceased).
> Chief Engineer George Rattray Scarth.
> Second Engineer Harry Arnold.
> Fourth Engineer Herbert Waugh.
> Junior Engineer Henry Hawkes.
> Electrician Frederick Reginald Hughes.
> Able Seaman William Howard Vincent.
> Able Seaman Charles James Percy Shaw (deceased).
> Able Seaman Douglas William Southgate (deceased)

5

During the last three months of 1944 the Germans were using their U-boats with great circumspection. Submarines fitted with Schnorkels were operating against our convoys to North Russia and in the coastal waters round the United Kingdom. Others of the ordinary type were at work off Canada and the east coast of the United States, while apart from the Japanese there were five or six German U-boats working from Penang and Batavia. December saw a sharp recrudescence of submarine activity in the English Channel, where five merchant ships and a frigate were sunk and three other vessels damaged. The Blue Star *Empire Javelin* was one of the merchant ships lost.

The first quarter of 1945 still saw 50 to 60 U-boats operating, some in the Arctic, others off Halifax, Nova Scotia, and in the western approaches to the Straits of Gibraltar, and still more in the Irish Sea. The so-called " Midget " submarines were working in the North Sea and Channel, though not with any great success. In April the enemy still had more than 200 U-boats for operations all over the world, of which 72 were still at sea. But their losses were colossal, for in that month alone 33 were destroyed at sea by surface or air forces, and another 24 through other causes, either minefields or bombing.

The end of the great drama was in sight, though three Allied merchant ships were sunk during May before the German surrender became effective. The last two of these merchantmen were sunk a few hours before the capitulation within a mile of May Island, at the entrance to the Firth of Forth, by one of the new type U-boats with high submerged speed.

Germany's capitulation was signed at Rheims on the night of May 6th-7th. Up till then the month of May saw another 25 U-boats destroyed in action. Most of these kills were carried out by aircraft in Danish waters through which U-boats were streaming in a *sauve qui peut* to Norway. Very few escaped.

Soon after 4.0 p.m. on May 4th, Grand Admiral Doenitz had sent a wireless signal to all U-boats at sea to cease hostilities and return to their bases. At noon on May 8th the Admiralty announced that the German High Command had been ordered to command all the U-boats at sea to come to the surface, hoist black flags, report in plain language their numbers and positions, and proceed by fixed routes to designated ports and anchorages.

The first U-boat to obey, U-249, surfaced off the Lizard on May 9th, and was escorted to Portland. U-532 surfaced near the Faeroe Islands on May 10th, and was sent to Loch Erribol. She carried a cargo from Japan of 601 tons of rubber, 110 tons of tin, 8 tons of wolfram, 5 tons of molybdenum and half-a-ton of quinine. On May 14th, seven U-boats, which had been escorted from Loch Erribol, surrendered off Lissahally, Northern Ireland. On May 16th a Norwegian destroyer, on passage to Narvik, met a convoy of 15 U-boats escorted by five surface ships. The submarines were escorted to Loch Erribol by the ships of a Canadian escort group.

Up till May 31st 49 U-boats had surrendered at sea. By mid-September, at which time a fuller, though not necessarily final account was possible, 156 German submarines had been surrendered to the Allies and another 221 were found to have been scuttled or destroyed by their crews. In all a total of 781 German U-boats were sunk or destroyed during the war.

6

Let us never forget the part played by our Merchant Seamen in the greatest maritime war of all time, and the war in which we most narrowly escaped defeat. The U-boats were not the only enemies with which they had to contend. There were also the enemy aircraft, the mines and the raiders, of which I have given some figures in the Introduction to this book, and here and there throughout the narrative. In the Introduction I have also mentioned the 30,000 British merchant seamen who gave their lives that Britain might live.

And what of the future?

In spite of the advent and rapidly-increasing carrying capacity of aircraft, the British Empire still remains an Oceanic Commonwealth of free nations linked together by the sea, and will so remain for some time to come. As I see it, too, the British Empire in its strength, and the friendship and unity of purpose of the two great English-speaking communities, the United States of America and ourselves, are the two greatest guarantees for the future peace of the world and the safety of civilization.

I cannot follow the argument that the atomic bomb has altered the importance of Sea Power, however much it may alter the type of ships. Britain herself still remains an over-crowded industrial island, dependent upon ships for by far the greatest proportion of her food, the raw materials for her industries, the export of coal which is our only natural resource, and the re-export of finished products for oversea markets. Without ships we cannot exist, and Sea Power is built up not only in warships ; but in merchant ships as well.

In 1638 John Hollond wrote what he called his first ' Discourse of the Navy.' It was a period when, though there were regular warships, the line of demarcation between them and merchantmen was not so hard-and-fast as it is now. Merchant-men were used as warships during hostilities, and in referring to " the Navy " John Hollond was referring to shipping of every kind.

158

This is what he wrote, which is as true today as it ever was :

" If either the honour of a nation, commerce or trade with all nations, peace at home, grounded upon our enemies' fear or love of us abroad, and attended with plenty of all things necessary either for the preservation of the public need or thy private welfare, be things worthy thy esteem (though it may be beyond thy shoal conceit), then next to God and the King give thy thanks for the same to the navy, as the principal instrument whereby God works these good things to thee. As for honour, who knows not (that know's anything) that in all records of late times of actions chronicled to the everlasting fame and renown of this kingdom, still the naval part is the thread that runs through the whole wooft, the binder of the song, the scope of the text ? "

THE END.

APPENDIX I

BLUE STAR LINE

SEAFARING PERSONNEL LOST AT SEA THROUGH ENEMY ACTION 1939 TO 1945.

Name	Rank	Name	Rank
Abbott, R. ..	.. Chief Steward.	Brooke, L. ..	.. Refrig. Greaser.
Abrahams, A.	.. Asst. Steward.	Brookes, A...	.. A.B. Seaman.
Adair, J. ..	.. A.B. Seaman.	Brookes, W...	.. Asst. Steward.
Adams, G. ..	.. Carpenter.	Brown, A. ..	.. Refrig. Greaser.
Aitken, G. ..	.. Galley Boy.	Brown, A ..	.. Fireman.
Allan, G. ..	.. Asst. Steward.	Brown, C. E.	.. ChiefRefrig.Engineer.
Allen, A. ..	.. Donkeyman Greaser.	Brown, G. ..	.. A.B. Seaman.
Allen, F. T...	.. Surgeon.	Brown, J. K.	.. Scullion.
Almond, C...	.. ChiefRefrig.Engineer.	Brown, R. ..	.. Galley Boy.
Alton, J. ..	.. Chief W.T.O.	Browne, J. ..	.. Donkeyman Greaser.
Anderson, T.	.. Fireman.	Bruce, J. ..	.. Carpenter's Mate.
Armstrong, J.	.. Bed. Steward.	Bryant, V. J.	.. A.B. Seaman.
Arris, A. ..	.. A.B. Seaman.	Bryde, R. ..	.. Main Greaser.
Ashworth, J.	.. 3rd Officer.	Buckwell, E.	.. Chief Engineer.
Atkins, H. ..	.. Asst. Engineer.	Budd, J. ..–	.. Bed. Steward.
Austin, W. ..	.. 3rd Engineer.	Buddell, M...	.. 4th Officer.
Auty, G. W.	.. Chief Engineer.	Burke, P. ..	.. A.B. Seaman.
Ayling, P. ..	.. Cadet.	Burling, W...	.. 3rd Engineer.
Bache, A. ..	.. Asst. Cook.	Burton, J. ..	.. A.B. Seaman.
Baggs, A. ..	.. Main Greaser.	Byrne, P. ..	.. Donkeyman Greaser.
Baggs, F. ..	.. Refrig. Greaser.	Cadogan, J...	.. Night Watch.
Baldwin, D...	.. Main Greaser.	Caliste, C. ..	.. Trimmer.
Balestrine, L.	.. Chief Cook.	Calloway, R.	.. Asst. Steward.
Barrett, J. ..	.. Kitchen Boy.	Camilleri, W.	.. Asst. Steward.
Bartels, C. ..	.. Trimmer.	Caminow, J.	.. Eng. Stores.
Bates, W. ..	.. Refrig. Greaser.	Campbell, J.	.. Quarter Master.
Bayne, H. ..	.. Trimmer.	Campbell, P.	.. 3rd Engineer.
Belford, W...	.. 2nd Engineer.	Capon, S. N.	.. Master.
Bell, G. T. ..	.. Refrig. Greaser.	Carter, O. ..	.. Lamptrimmer.
Benbow, A...	.. Cadet.	Carton, W. ..	.. 3/W.T.O.
Benbow (Miss), G...	Shop Asst.	Cartwright, J.	.. Asst. Steward.
Benn, J. ..	.. Refrig. Greaser.	Castell, W. E.	.. Pantry Boy.
Bevan, W. ..	.. Asst. Steward.	Cavanna, J...	.. Asst. Cook.
Black, D. ..	.. Steward's Boy.	Cave, W. C.	.. A.B. Seaman.
Blackwood, R.	.. Refrig. Greaser.	Cavell, N. V.	.. Chief W.T.O.
Blandford, H.	.. Chief Engineer.	Cawthorne, R.	.. Donkeyman Greaser.
Blatcher, R.	.. A.B. Seaman.	Chapman, H.	.. Bosun's Mate.
Bleasdale, H.	.. Asst. Steward.	Cheers, A. ..	.. A.B. Seaman.
Bloomer, C. C.	.. Chief Steward.	Christie, A...	.. Chief Electrician.
Bowden, H...	.. Asst. Engineer.	Christie, T...	.. Donkeyman Greaser.
Bowers, S. ..	.. Junior 4th Engineer.	Christodoulos, B.	.. Main Greaser.
Bowles, H. ..	.. Chief Cook.	Clark, C. ..	.. Fireman.
Boyle, M. ..	.. Refrig. Greaser.	Clark, W. ..	.. Kitchen Boy.
Bradshaw, W.	.. Asst. Steward.	Clarke, W. ..	.. 3rd Engineer.
Branch, T. ..	.. Fireman	Clegg, H. ..	.. Purser.
Brandie, W...	.. ChiefRefrig.Engineer.	Clyde, S. ..	.. Asst. Steward.
Brassey, H...	.. Asst. Steward.	Coalthorpe, A.	.. Refrig. Greaser.
Brewer, A. ..	.. Quarter Master.	Coates, S. ..	.. Fireman.
Briegal, J. ..	.. Kitchen Boy.	Cochrane, J.	.. 2nd Cook.
Brindley, J...	.. Bosun's Mate.	Cockett, G...	.. Main Greaser.
Brito, P. ..	.. Donkeyman Greaser.	Cockran, P...	.. Donkeyman Greaser.
Brook, D. ..	.. Writer.	Cocks, W. ..	.. 2nd Cook.

Name	Rank	Name	Rank
Collins, J.	Carpenter.	Findlay, W.	A.B. Seaman.
Conn, B.	Asst. Steward.	Finn, C.	Fireman.
Connor, S.	Steward's Boy.	Firth, T.	Steward's Boy.
Cook, J.	Bosun.	Fisher, J.	Master.
Copeman, T.	2nd Electrician.	Fitzsimmons, C.	Fireman.
Corfield, E.	Main Greaser.	Fleisher, A.	Asst. Baker.
Cornish, A. J.	Purser.	Flood, W.	Fireman.
Costello, P.	Asst. Steward.	Forbes, J.	2nd Refrig. Engineer.
Coughlan, J.	Cadet.	Forrest, T.	Asst. Engineer.
Cousins, R.	Scullion.	Forster, J.	Donkeyman Greaser.
Crist, T.	Main Greaser.	Francis, R.	Chief Engineer.
Crossman, T.	Refrig. Greaser.	Frazer, G.	Trimmer.
Crown, G.	Quarter Master.	Freckleton, A.	Asst. Steward.
Cullis, J.	Refrig. Greaser.	Gain, A.	Ship's Cook.
Cummings, M.	Carpenter.	Gain, B.	Laundry Man.
Cundey, R.	4th Engineer.	Gall, A.	2nd Engineer.
Cunningham, H.	Fireman.	Gallagher, P.	Steward's Boy.
Currell, J.	A.B. Seaman.	Galvin, E.	Storekeeper.
Daracott, B.	Fireman.	Gannon, H.	Fireman.
Davies, E.	Fireman.	Gannon, L.	Fireman.
Davies, F. W.	3/W.T.O.	Gassey, J.	Asst. Steward.
Davies, H.	Pantry Boy.	Gee, J.	Asst. Engineer.
Davies, L.	Fireman.	George, W.	Trimmer.
Davies, R.	A.B. Seaman.	Gerrard, M.	Fireman.
Davies, W.	Junior 4th Engineer.	Gibbons, M.	Donkeyman Greaser.
Davis, J.	Chief Electrician.	Gill, R.	Chief Officer.
Davis, J.	Chief Officer.	Girdler, R.	Asst. Engineer.
Dawson (Miss), H.	Stewardess.	Godfrey, J.	Asst. Engineer.
Delaney, J.	Refrig. Greaser.	Godley, J.	A.B. Seaman.
Demowetta, L.	Trimmer.	Gogarthy, J.	A.B. Seaman.
Dennis, F.	Pantry Boy.	Gomes, M.	Fireman.
Dennison, W.	Greaser.	Good, F.	A.B. Seaman.
Depas, H.	Fireman.	Goodman, J.	Quarter Master.
Desson, C.	Greaser.	Gordon, W.	A.B. Seaman.
Dewey, I.	Baker.	Gostock, H.	A.B. Seaman.
Dickinson, R.	Donkeyman Greaser.	Goulding, J.	Asst. Engineer.
Doe, G.	Trimmer.	Grace, B.	Laundry Boy.
Dolan, P.	Main Greaser.	Grace, H. H.	2nd Officer.
Dowdall, H.	Donkeyman Greaser.	Grace, S.	Fireman.
Dove (Miss), E.	Shop Asst.	Gray, A. D.	Chief Engineer.
Draper, A.	A.B. Seaman.	Gray, J.	A.B. Seaman.
Drew, J.	O.S.	Grayson, R.	2/W.T.O.
Dudgeon, E.	Chief Electrician.	Green, A.	A.B. Seaman.
Duggin, G.	A.B. Seaman.	Green, (Mrs.) L.	Stewardess.
Dunnell, G.	Steward's Boy.	Green, R.	4th Officer.
Dunville, R.	3rd Engineer.	Greenwood, A.	A.B. Seaman.
East, E.	Chief Refrig. Engineer.	Griffiths, W. D.	Quarter Master.
Eaton, J.	Cook's Boy.	Griggs, E.	2nd Engineer.
Edgecombe, F.	Asst. Steward.	Grigor, J.	Carpenter.
Edmonds, J. H.	3rd Officer.	Gudgin, T.	Master.
Ellen, B.	Quarter Master.	Gunther, C.	Eng. Stores
Elliott, J.	2nd Officer.	Hague, W.	A.B. Seaman.
Elliott, O.	Butcher.	Haizeldene, L.	Fireman.
Ellis, C.	Main Greaser.	Hall, A. G.	Cadet.
Ellis, T.	Asst. Steward.	Hall, J. B.	Master.
Elsey, F.	Asst. Steward.	Halson, W.	Pantry-Man.
Evans, A.	Deck Boy.	Halson, J. M.	Scullion.
Evans, A.	Fireman.	Halson, W. T.	Asst. Cook.
Evans, J.	Asst. Steward.	Hamilton, G.	Donkeyman Greaser.
Evans, O.	Asst. Steward.	Hamilton, J.	2nd Engineer.
Evans, T.	A.B. Seaman.	Hammond, T.	Quarter Master.
Evans, T.	Chief Electrician.	Hampson, E.	Asst. Steward.
Farquahar, J.	Asst. Steward.	Harcourt, R.	Barman.

Name	Rank	Name	Rank
Hargan, N...	Cook's Boy.	Johnston, C.	Fireman.
Harris, H. ..	Confectioner.	Johnston, J...	A.B. Seaman.
Harris, P. ..	Chief W.T.O.	Johnston, L.	Asst. Steward.
Harrison, J...	Asst. Steward.	Jones, C. ..	Asst. Engineer.
Hart, C. ..	Lamptrimmer.	Jones, C. ..	Fireman.
Hartley, L. ..	Fireman.	Jones, E. ..	A.B. Seaman.
Harvey, A. ..	Bosun.	Jones, H. ..	Bedroom Steward.
Hasline, C...	Junior 4th Engineer.	Jones, J. W...	A.B. Seaman.
Hastings, L.	Eng. Stores.	Jones, N. ..	Cadet.
Hatton, J. H.	2/W.T.O.	Jones, R. ..	Kitchen Boy.
Haugh, J. ..	2nd Refrig. Engineer.	Jones, R. ..	Donkeyman Greaser.
Haughey, J.	A.B. Seaman.	Jones, T. ..	Fireman.
Hayes, R. ..	Asst. Steward.	Jorgenson, B.	3rd Engineer.
Hayles, W. E.	Asst. Steward.	Kane, J. ..	A.B. Seaman.
Healey, J. ..	Eng. Stores.	Kavanagh, T.	Steward's Boy.
Hensall, C.	Asst. Engineer.	Kehoe, P. ..	Main Greaser.
Henshaw, S.	3rd Engineer.	Kehoe, R. ..	Fireman.
Herbert, G...	A.B. Seaman.	Kellegher, D.	Asst. Steward.
Heyburn, L.	Quarter Master.	Kelly, J. ..	Greaser.
Higgins, E...	Eng. Stores.	Kemp, H. ..	A.B. Seaman.
Highton, B...	2nd Officer	Kendall, W.	A.B. Seaman.
Hilditch, R.	Donkeyman Greaser.	Kendrew, G.	Chief Cook.
Hill, F. ..	Steward's Boy.	Kilpatrick, C.	Chief Engineer.
Hobson, J. W.	Asst. Steward.	King, L. E..	A.B. Seaman.
Hogan, G. ..	Main Greaser.	Kirkham, D.	2/W.T.O.
Hogg, F. S...	2nd Engineer.	Kjortsholtzen, A.	Fireman.
Holleron, M.	Main Greaser.	Kyte, J. J. ..	A.B. Seaman.
Hollings, F.	3/W.T.O.	Laing, L. ...	Trimmer.
Holohan, F.	Asst. Steward.	Lambert, G.	Baker.
Holt, L. ..	Asst. Steward.	Lannon, J. ..	Main Greaser.
Hooper, R...	Donkeyman Greaser.	Larkin, J. ..	Fireman.
Hough, T. ..	Quarter Master.	Larsen, C. ..	Asst. Engineer.
Howard, H. C.	Master.	Latimer, R...	A.B. Seaman.
Hudson, J. ..	Asst. Steward.	Lawrence, W. M. ..	Fireman.
Hudson, R...	Asst. Steward.	Lawrenson, J.	Quarter Master.
Hughes, A. ..	A.B. Seaman.	Lawson, T. ...	Main Greaser.
Hughes, G. P.	Purser.	Leay, E. ..	Steward's Boy.
Hughes, J. ..	Asst. Engineer.	Leckie, T. ..	2/W.T.O.
Hughes, J. ..	Fireman.	Leech, G. ..	2nd Refrig. Engineer.
Hughes, T. ..	2nd Steward.	Lees, G. ..	4th Engineer.
Hughes, T. ..	Donkeyman Greaser.	Lemon, C. ..	Asst. Engineer.
Humphries, L.	2nd Cook.	Lester, N. ..	Linen Keeper.
Hunter, W...	Asst. Steward.	Leuchars, W. S.	Chief W.T.O.
Hutchins, W.	Steward's Boy.	Lever, A. ..	Deck Steward.
Hutchinson, R.	Writer.	Lewis, A. ..	Deck Boy.
Hutton, F. ..	Writer.	Lewis, C. H.	Chief Officer.
Hynes, J. ..	Asst. Butcher.	Lewis, J. ..	Trimmer.
Ingham, R...	Asst. Steward.	Lewis, T. O.	Chief Electrician.
Inskip, R. ..	2nd Steward.	Liddle, R. T.	4th Officer.
Jackson, A...	3/W.T.O.	Llewellyn, W.	A.B. Seaman.
Jackson, G...	A.B. Seaman.	Locatelli, P.	Cadet.
Jackson, G...	A.B. Seaman.	Lofts, E. ..	Asst. Cook.
Jackson, P. ..	Cadet.	Lounig, N. ..	4th Officer.
Jackson, R...	Stores.	Loveridge, D.	Deck Boy.
Jallow, A. R.	Fireman.	Lunne, C. ..	Bedroom Steward.
Jarman, R. ..	A.B. Seaman.	Lyness, H. ..	Asst. Steward.
Jenkins, P. ..	Fireman.	McArcle, P.	Fireman.
Jocobsen, C.	Asst. Steward.	McArde, P...	Fireman.
John, S. ..	Fireman.	McAthey, W.	Asst. Steward.
Johnson, D.	Steward's Boy	McCafferty, G.	A.B. Seaman.
Johnson, J. ..	Trimmer.	McCall, J. ..	Asst. Engineer.
Johnson, K...	Greaser.	McCarne, P.	Greaser.
Johnson, W.	Chief Steward.	McCarthy, J.	Greaser.

Name	Rank
McClellan, E.	.. Barkeeper.
McCuaig, D.	.. A.B. Seaman.
McGarry, J.	.. Chief Cook.
McGovern, P.	.. O.S.
McGuiness, T.	.. Donkeyman Greaser.
McIndow, C.	.. Asst. Cook.
McKenna, J.	.. Refrig. Greaser.
McMahon, R.	.. Fireman.
McManse, T.	.. Refrig. Greaser.
McMillan, R.	.. Main Greaser.
McNally, H.	.. Asst. Steward.
McNamee J.	.. Refrig. Greaser.
McNeil, T. ..	.. A.B. Seaman.
McNulty, H.	.. Chief Cook.
McPherson, G.	.. Chief Officer.
McWilliam, G.	.. Lamptrimmer.
McAuley, J.	.. Fireman.
McDonald, R.	.. Asst. Steward.
McKillican, S.	.. 3rd Officer.
McKinnon, D.	.. A.B. Seaman.
McLean, A...	.. Asst. Engineer.
McSherry, D.	.. Doctor.
McCoy, J. ..	.. Chief Steward.
Mack, H. ..	.. Chief Cook.
Mackie, J. ..	.. Bed. Steward.
Mahoney, J.	.. A.B. Seaman.
Mann, J.	.. Asst. Steward.
Marney, J. ...	.. Donkeyman Greaser.
Marsh, C. ..	.. Chief Refrig. Engineer.
Marshall, D.	.. Bosun's Mate.
Marshall, T. H.	.. 4th Officer.
Martin, J. ..	.. Steward's Boy.
Martin, J. ..	.. S/Asst. Steward.
Martin, M. ..	.. Asst. Steward.
Massouda, H.	.. Junior 4th Engineer.
Matthews, R.	.. A.B. Seaman.
May, W. ..	.. Junior 4th Engineer.
Mecham, F.	.. Fireman.
Meek, E. ..	.. 3/W.T.O.
Mensah, J. ..	.. Fireman.
Mercer, L. ..	.. Kitchen Boy.
Michaels, J...	.. Steward's Boy.
Midgeley, J.	.. 2nd Engineer.
Miller, J. ..	.. A.B. Seaman.
Miller, R. D.	.. Master.
Mills, J. ..	.. Master.
Mitchell, F...	.. Asst. Engineer.
Moitie, W...	.. Night Watchman.
Monod, E. ..	.. Asst. Steward.
Monson, J. ..	.. Lamptrimmer.
Montgomery, W.	.. Fireman/Trimmer.
Moon, J. ..	.. Asst. Engineer.
Mooney, J. ..	.. Fireman.
Moore, G. ..	.. Butcher.
Moore, H. ..	.. Fireman.
Moore, J. ..	.. Fireman.
Moorhead, J.	.. Fireman.
Morey, R. J.	.. Chief Steward.
Morgan, D. L.	.. Steward's Boy.
Morgan, L...	.. Steward's Boy.
Morris, H. ..	.. Fireman/Trimmer.
Mortimer, B.	.. A.B. Seaman.
Moulton, E. W.	.. Master.

Name	Rank
Moulini, P. ...	.. Chief Cook.
Mowatt, A. R.	.. Asst. Engineer.
Mudkins, A.	.. 2nd Cook.
Mulcahy, J...	.. Junior 4th Engineer.
Mulvey, G. ...	.. Scullion.
Mullen, R. ...	.. Donkeyman Greaser.
Munro, A. ..	.. 3rd Engineer.
Murphy, E...	.. Fireman.
Murphy, H.	.. Fireman.
Murphy, M.	.. Asst. Steward.
Murphy, P...	.. A.B. Seaman.
Myers, A. ..	.. Fireman.
Nash, R. ..	.. Asst. Steward.
Nealon, P. ..	.. 4th Officer.
Nelson, T. ..	.. Refrig. Greaser.
Newman, T.	.. Asst. Steward.
North, A. ..	.. Silverman.
Norton, R. ..	.. Carpenter's Mate.
Nylander, W.	.. Carpenter.
O'Connor, F.	.. O.S.
O'Connor, H.	.. Chief Steward.
Oliver, J. ..	.. A.B. Seaman.
Omofaiye, T.	.. Greaser.
O'Neill, C. ..	.. A.B. Seaman.
O'Neill, J. ..	.. Deck Boy.
O'Reilly, J...	.. Asst. Cook.
Orger, L. ..	.. Asst. Steward.
Owen, J. ..	.. Asst. Engineer.
Owen, W. ..	.. A.B. Seaman.
Palmer, J. ..	.. Quarter Master.
Parker, E. ..	.. A.B. Seaman.
Parsonage, P. M.	.. 4th Officer.
Parsons, L. ..	.. Chief Officer.
Patterson, A.	.. Asst. Steward.
Patterson, G.	.. Cadet.
Pearce, W. ..	.. Fireman.
Pearkson, W.	.. Carpenter.
Pearman, F.	.. Bosun.
Pedersen, P.	.. Doctor.
Pendleton, W.	.. Fireman/Trimmer.
Pennock, C.	.. Kitchen Boy.
Percival, W.	.. 2nd Electrician.
Percival, W.	.. Asst. Steward.
Perry, R. ..	.. Cadet.
Peter, B. ..	.. Fireman.
Peters, H. ..	.. Fireman.
Peters, N. ..	.. Fireman.
Pettigrew, W.	.. Asst. Engineer.
Phillips, J. ..	.. Fireman.
Pilkington, J.	.. Main Greaser.
Pimlett, P. ..	.. Asst. Steward.
Pitkin, J. A.	.. A.B. Seaman.
Pittuck, G. ..	.. Chief Cook.
Plank, J. E...	.. Chief Cook.
Plummer, J.	.. Asst. Cook.
Pontus, J. ..	.. Scullion.
Porteous, J...	.. Chief W.T.O.
Power, W. ..	.. Bosun.
Prestige, L. ...	.. Steward's Boy.
Prickett, E. O.	.. Chief Officer.
Pye, E. ..	.. 4th Engineer.
Pike, J. ..	.. Fireman.
Quingley, G.	.. Chief W.T.O.

Name	Rank	Name	Rank
Quinn, J. P.	Pantry Boy.	Stander, C.	Asst. Steward.
Rabinowitz, P.	Scullion.	Standing, W. B.	Fireman.
Rackham, L.	3rd Officer.	Stanley, F.	Bed. Steward.
Rafferty, F.	Fireman.	Stephens, F.	Asst. Steward.
Ranson, L.	A.B. Seaman.	Stevenson, J.	A.B. Seaman.
Ranson, S.	2nd Officer.	Steward, C.	Pantry Boy.
Rawlings, J.	Scullion.	Stewart, A.	Bosun.
Reath, W.	O.S.	Stewart, R.	Chief W.T.O.
Reay, L.	A.B. Seaman.	Strode, J.	A.B. Seaman.
Reddin, J.	A.B. Seaman.	Studholme, A.	Fireman.
Reekie, D.	Asst. Engineer.	Sullivan, J.	2/W.T.O.
Ribbons, C.	Chief Steward.	Suncksum, A.	Fireman/Trimmer.
Rice, H.	A.B. Seaman.	Sutcliffe, C.	3/W.T.O.
Richards, W. E.	Chief Officer.	Swain, H.	Asst. Steward.
Rigby, S.	Bosun.	Swanson, F.	Storekeeper.
Rippon, S.	4th Engineer.	Swanson, N.	Refrig. Greaser.
Roache, P.	Fireman.	Swanwick, E.	Silverman.
Roberts, E.	Asst. Cook.	Tarrant, W.	Fireman.
Roberts, J.	Asst. Steward.	Taylor, G.	Eng. Stores.
Roberts, L.	Asst. Steward.	Teaney, M.	Main Greaser.
Roberts, T.	Refrig. Greaser.	Thompson, A.	A.B. Seaman.
Roberts, W. G.	Chief Refrig. Engineer.	Thompson, J.	Fireman.
Robinson, D.	3rd Officer	Thompson, W. S.	Fireman.
Robinson, R.	2/W.T.O.	Thomson, C.	Chief Refrig. Engineer.
Robson, T.	Asst. Engineer.	Thoseby, J.	Cadet.
Rodrigquez, P.	Asst. Steward.	Timms, W.	Laundry.
Rowland, A.	2/W.T.O.	Tinmouth, E.	Cook and Baker.
Romaine, J.	Donkeyman Greaser.	Tinniswood, S.	A.B. Seaman.
Rosier, A.	Chief Cook.	Tinton, B.	O.S.
Ross, A. T.	2/W.T.O.	Towers, A.	Asst. Engineer.
Rowan (Miss), M.	Stewardess.	Treliving, T.	2nd Engineer.
Rowaski, C.	Deck Boy.	Trillo, B.	4th Officer.
Rushton, I.	Chief Refrig. Engineer.	Turnbull, N.	Chief Refrig. Engineer.
Ryan, C.	Asst. Steward.	Turner, S.	Fireman.
Ryan, O.	Steward's Boy.	Turton, R.	Quarter Master.
Sankoh, H.	Fireman.	Tye, E.	4th Engineer.
Schofield, H.	Main Greaser.	Van-Der-Auwera, J.	Carpenter.
Schofield, E.	Asst. Steward.	Vella, G.	Fireman.
Scott, R.	O.S.	Vennils, S.	Lounge Steward.
Scrymgeor, S.	3rd Engineer.	Vincent, G.	Fireman.
Seagor, A.	A.B. Seaman.	Vincent, K.	2nd Electrician.
Seakie, A.	Asst. Steward.	Vine, E.	Bosun's Mate.
Senior, H. T.	3rd Officer.	Wagstaff, U.	Refrig. Greaser.
Sharkey, E.	Main Greaser.	Waldron, J. D.	Junior 3rd Engineer.
Sharpe, R. R.	Pantry Boy.	Walker, D.	Greaser.
Shaw, C.	A.B. Seaman.	Walker, J.	2nd Cook.
Sheehan, P.	A.B. Seaman.	Walker, J. D.	Asst. Engineer.
Shiel, J.	2nd Refrig. Engineer.	Walmsley, D.	Asst. Cook.
Simms, R.	Donkeyman Greaser.	Ward, J.	A.B. Seaman.
Sinacola, R.	Main Greaser.	Walsh, E. N.	Chief Officer.
Smith, F.	Butcher.	Walsh, W.	Master.
Smith, G. S.	Asst. Cook.	Walton, F.	Printer.
Smith, L.	A.B. Seaman.	Waterson, J.	Chief Steward.
Smith, J.	A.B. Seaman.	Watkins, J.	3rd Engineer.
Smith, J. W.	Deck Boy.	Watson, G. A.	Baker.
Smith, M.	Deck Boy.	Watson, J.	Carpenter.
Smitton, G.	Fireman/Trimmer.	Watt, G. W.	Chief Engineer.
Someone, J.	Fireman/Trimmer.	Watts, C.	Cadet.
Southgate, D.	A.B. Seaman.	Waugh, R.	Refrig. Greaser.
Speedy, P.	Fireman.	Weaver, E.	Trimmer.
Spencer, J.	Fireman.	Webb, E.	Refrig. Greaser.
Spencer, T.	O.S.	Webb, J.	Printer.
Spooner, R.	Fireman.	Webster, G.	Junior 4th Engineer.

Name	Rank	Name	Rank
Webster, J. V.	.. Asst. Cook.	Wilson, J. ..	.. 3rd Engineer.
Welch, H. ..	.. Senior Asst. Steward.	Wilson, R. ..	.. Asst. Engineer.
Wemyss, E...	.. Trimmer.	Wilson, W. ..	.. Asst. Cook.
Weston, H. ..	.. Purser.	Winsor, P. ..	.. Chief W.T.O.
Wheatley, A.	.. Laundry Boy.	Wisdom, W. H.	.. A.B. Seaman.
Whipp, E. ..	.. Asst. Engineer.	Witham, S. A.	.. Chief W.T.O.
White, S. ..	.. 3rd Engineer.	Wood, A. ..	.. Senior Asst. Steward.
Whitehead, R. G.	.. Master.	Wooding, R. J.	.. 3/W.T.O.
Whittington, J.	.. Fireman.	Woods, B. ..	.. Asst. Steward.
Wiggins, R. G.	.. Asst. Engineer.	Worth, G. V.	.. 4th Officer.
Wilkinson, H.	.. Bosun.		
Williams, A.	.. A.B. Seaman.	Young, A. ..	.. 2nd Steward.
Williams, D.	.. Fireman.	Young, G. ..	.. Galley Boy.
Williams, J. H.	.. Butcher.	Young, R. ..	.. 3rd Officer.
Williams, R.	.. Fireman.	Young, R. ..	.. A.B. Seaman.
Williams, S...	.. Asst. Steward.	Young, T. ..	.. Master.
Williams, S...	.. Asst. Steward.	Young, T. ..	.. Chief Engineer.
Willis, A. ..	.. 2nd Officer.		
Wilson, E. ..	.. Asst. Steward.	Zammit, F...	.. Fireman.
		Zammit, J...	.. Fireman.

Also 78 Gunners and 272 Passengers lost their lives.

APPENDIX II

BLUE STAR LINE

HONOURS LIST

NOTES.—Many of the names mentioned below appear also in the text.
Names in this list are not necessarily included in the Index.

Comm.=Commendation. Desp.=Mentioned in Despatches. (P)=Posthumous.

Name	Rank or Rating	Award	Ship or Service
C. W. ALMOND	.. Ch.Refrig.Eng.	Desp...	.. *Melbourne Star*. Malta Convoy.
L. N. ALLAN	.. Ch. Officer	.. Comm.	.. *Imperial Star*. Bombed in port.
J. L. ANSON	.. 2nd Officer	.. O.B.E.	.. *Avila Star*.
H. ARNOLD	.. 2nd Eng.	.. Comm.	.. *Empire Javelin*.
C. P. BARBER	.. A.B. ..	.. Comm.	.. *Empire Star*. Singapore.
W. BEST ..	.. Greaser	.. B.E.M.	.. *Melbourne Star*. Survivor.
N. BENNETT	.. A.B. ..	.. Comm.	.. *Andalucia Star*.
W. H. BEVAN	.. Capt. ..	.. Comm.	.. *Sultan Star*.
H. BLANDFORD	.. Ch. Eng.	.. D.S.C.	.. *Melbourne Star*. Malta Convoy.
F. BONES ..	.. Carpenter	.. B.E.M.	.. Long and meritorious service in M.N.
F. B. BROWN	.. Ch. Officer	.. Comm.	.. *Arandora Star*.
R. W. BROWN	.. Ch. Eng.	.. O.B.E.	.. Long and meritorious service in M.N.
E. G. BUCKWELL..	.. Ch. Eng.	.. Comm.	.. *Canadian Star*.
W. BURNS ..	.. Greaser	.. B.E.M.	.. *Melbourne Star*. Survivor.
S. N. CAPON	.. Capt. ..	.. C.B.E.	.. *Empire Star*. Singapore.
R. T. CLARKE	.. 3rd Officer	.. O.B.E.	.. *Avila Star*.
J. COOK ..	.. Bosun ..	.. D.S.M.	.. *Melbourne Star*. Malta Convoy.
B. C. CROOKS	.. Ch. Cook	.. B.E.M.	.. Long and meritorious service in M.N
J. A. CUCKSEY	.. Ch. Officer	.. Comm.	.. *Empire Javelin*.
J. L. DAWSON	.. Ch. Officer	.. O.B.E.	.. *Empire Star*. Singapore.
J. D. DEMPSTER ..	.. W/T Officer	.. Comm.	.. *Pacific Star*.
J. DOBBIE ..	.. 2nd Eng.	.. D.S.C.	.. *Brisbane Star*. Malta Convoy.
I. H. DONALDSON	A.B. ..	.. B.E.M.	.. *Empire Star*.
G. M. DUFF	.. Capt. ..	.. George Medal Lloyds Medal	*Empire Glade*.
G. L. EVANS	.. Capt. ..	.. O.B.E.	.. *Pacific Star*.
MARIA ELIZABETH FERGUSON	.. Passenger	.. B.E.M.	.. *Avila Star*.

Name	Rank or Rating	Award	Ship or Service
J. Fleming..	A.B. ..	D.S.M.	*Melbourne Star.* Malta Convoy.
R. Foulkner	Cadet ..	Comm.	*Empire Star.* Singapore.
R. F. Francis	Ch. Eng.	O.B.E.	*Empire Star.* Singapore.
A. D. Fraser	4th Eng.	Comm.	*Empire Might.*
A. E. Fry..	A.B. ..	B.E.M.	*Afric Star.*
W. C. Goody	Naval Gunner	B.E.M.	*Canadian Star.*
J. D. Golightly..	2nd Officer	M.B.E.	*Empire Star.* Singapore.
F. W. Gordon	Ch. Steward..	Comm.	*Imperial Star.*
J. A. Gray	Bosun ..	B.E.M.	*Avila Star.*
Mrs. L. A. Green	Stewardess	Comm. (P)	*Andalucia Star.*
A. Greenwood	A.B. ..	D.S.M.	*Melbourne Star.* Malta Convoy.
G. Haig ..	Ch. Eng.	O.B.E. ..⎫ Lloyds Medal⎰	*Sydney Star.* Malta Convoy.
J. B. Hall	Capt. ..	Comm.	*Andalucia Star.*
H. C. Hawkes	Asst. Eng.	Comm.	*Empire Javelin.*
H. E. Heaver	Donkeyman ..	Comm.	*Empire Star.* Singapore.
A. C. Hender	2nd Officer	M.B.E.	*Empire Glade.*
T. S. Horn	Capt. ..	O.B.E. ..⎫ Lloyds Medal⎰	*Sydney Star.* Malta Convoy.
C. R. Horton	2nd Officer	D.S.C.	*Brisbane Star.* Malta Convoy.
J. W. Hubbard	4th Eng.	Comm.	*Andalucia Star.*
F. R. Hughes	2nd Electrician	Comm.	*Empire Javelin.*
T. S. Hughes	2nd Steward..	Comm.	*Empire Star.* Singapore.
P. H. Hunt	Ch. Officer	Comm. ..⎫ M.B.E. ⎰	*Canadian Star.*
J. W. Innes	Ch. Eng.	Comm. ..⎫ O.B.E. ..⎰	*Royal Star.* Long and meritorious service in M.N.
G. G. D. C. Jackson	2nd Steward..	Comm.	*Imperial Star.* Ship bombed in port.
F. N. Johnson	Ch. Officer	M.B.E.	*Dunedin Star.*
J. J. Johnson	2nd Eng.	Comm.	*Empire Star.* Singapore.
W. S. Johnstone..	Capt. (Passenger)..	Comm.	*Canadian Star.*
C. J. W. Jones	Capt. ..	Comm.	*Canadian Star.*
D. C. Keenliside	2nd Eng.	M.B.E.	*Empire Glade.*
R. H. Keyworth	3rd Officer	M.B.E.	*Canadian Star.*
G. D. Knight	3rd Officer	M.B.E.	*Melbourne Star.* Malta Convoy.
I. A. B. Knight..	Naval Gunner	Comm.	*Sydney Star.* Malta Convoy.
H. Kuhlman	Bosun ..	B.E.M.	*Andalucia Star.* Long and meritorious service in M.N.
C. S. Low..	Capt. (Passenger)..	Comm.	*Avila Star.*
D. R. MacFarlane	Capt. ..	O.B.E. ..⎫ D.S.O. ..⎰	*Melbourne Star.* Malta Convoys.
J. H. A. Mackie..	Capt. ..	M.B.E. ..⎫ Lloyds Medal⎬ O.B.E. ..⎭	*Sydney Star.* Malta Convoy. *Celtic Star.*
A. A. MacKinnon	Bosun ..	Comm.	*Royal Star.*
F. MacQuiston	Ch. Officer	M.B.E.	*Viking Star.*
T. F. McDonald	Capt. ..	O.B.E. ..⎫ Lloyds Medal⎰	*Royal Star.*
J. McLean	Capt. ..	Comm.	*Empire Javelin.*
J. McMillan	A.B. ..	B.E.M.	*California Star.*
H. McNeilly	Engine Room Storekeeper ..	Desp...	Malta Convoy.
F. McWilliam	Lamptrimmer	D.S.M.	*Melbourne Star.* Malta Convoy.
J. Middleton	3rd Eng.	Comm.	*Empire Star.* Singapore.
D. R. Miller	Capt. ..	Comm. (P)	*Canadian Star.*
S. Milne ..	Carpenter	B.E.M.	*Empire Star.* Singapore.
J. R. Mitchell	3rd Eng.	Comm.	*Empire Star.* Singapore.
R. Moscrop-Young	3rd Officer	M.B.E.	*Empire Star.*
E. W. Moulton..	Capt. ..	Comm. (P)	*Arandora Star.*
J. Murphy	W/T Officer	Comm.	*Celtic Star.*

Name	Rank or Rating	Award	Ship or Service
H. NANCHOLAS	Engine Room Storekeeper	B.E.M.	*Gaelic Star.* Long and meritorious service in M.N.
A. R. NICOL	Ch. Eng.	D.S.C.	*Brisbane Star.* Malta Convoy.
R. NUNN	O.S.	B.E.M.	*Melbourne Star.* Survivor.
J. NUTTALL	3rd Eng.	M.B.E.	*Celtic Star.*
A. NYLANDER	Carpenter	D.S.M.	*Brisbane Star.* Malta Convoy.
H. O'CONNOR	Ch. Steward	D.S.M.	*Melbourne Star.* Malta Convoy.
L. OLDHAM	Asst. Steward	B.E.M.	Long and meritorious service in M.N. Survivor of *Arandora Star*, 1940 ; *Avila Star*, 1942 ; *Empire Star*, 1942).
G. OWEN	Capt.	O.B.E.	*Dunedin Star.* Malta Convoy.
J. B. PARKER	Ch. Eng.	O.B.E.	*Empire Glade.*
L. PARSONS	Ch. Officer	D.S.C.	*Melbourne Star.* Malta Convoy.
E. R. PEARCE	Ch. Officer	O.B.E. Lloyds Medal	*Avila Star.*
E. O. PEDERSEN	Surgeon	Comm. (P)	*California Star.*
R. PERRY	Cadet	Comm.	*Empire Star.* Singapore.
S. J. C. PHILLIPS	Capt.	Comm. C.B.E.	*Empire Might.* Long and meritorious service in M.N.
E. D. POWELL	Engineer	O.B.E.	*Gaelic Star.* Long and meritorious service in M.N.
G. POWELL	Ch. Steward	B.E.M.	*Trojan Star.* Long and meritorious service in M.N.
W. POWER	Bosun	B.E.M.	*Empire Star.* Singapore.
A. J. PRETTY	3rd Eng.	Desp.	*Brisbane Star.* Malta Convoy.
W. RAY	Ch. Eng.	O.B.E.	*Empire Strength.* Long and meritorious service in M.N.
C. E. RIBBONS	Ch. Steward	Comm.	*Empire Star.* Singapore.
W. E. RICHARDS	2nd Officer	Desp.	*Melbourne Star.* Malta Convoy.
F. N. RILEY	Capt.	D.S.O.	*Brisbane Star.* Malta Convoy.
G. ROBERTS	Ch. Officer	M.B.E.	*Empire Glade.*
A. J. ROBINSON	Naval Gunner	Comm.	*Sydney Star.*
O. C. ROBERTS	Capt.	C.B.E.	*Australia Star.* Long and meritorious service in M.N.
A. J. ROBINSON	Naval Gunner	Comm.	*Sydney Star.*
D. ROBINSON	3rd Officer	Comm. (P)	*Empire Javelin.*
G. R. SCARTH	Ch. Eng.	Comm.	*Empire Javelin.*
W. SHAKESHAFT	Carpenter	B.E.M.	*Empire Glade.*
C. J. P. SHAW	A.B.	Comm. (P)	*Empire Javelin.*
B. G. SHERRATT	2nd Eng.	Comm.	*Canadian Star.*
F. SIMMONS	Storekeeper	B.E.M.	*Empire Glade.*
J. P. SMITH	3rd Officer	M.B.E.	*Empire Star.* Singapore.
D. W. J. SOUTHGATE	A.B.	Comm. (P)	*Empire Javelin.*
R. STEWART	W/T Officer	Comm.	*California Star.*
D. J. STRATTA	Ch. Officer	Comm.	*Empire Might.*
A. R. SUTHERLAND	Carpenter	Comm.	*Avila Star.*
M. B. TALLACK	1st Officer	O.B.E.	*Avila Star.*
E. E. THOMAS	Ch. Officer	R.H.S. Certificate	Saving life in New York Harbour.
H. TOMLINSON	Ch. Eng.	O.B.E.	*Dunedin Star.* Malta Convoy.
L. VERNON	Ch. Officer	M.B.E.	*Empire Star.*
W. H. VINCENT	A.B.	Comm.	*Empire Javelin.*
H. WAUGH	4th Eng.	Comm.	*Empire Javelin.*
H. C. WELLER	2nd Eng.	M.B.E.	*Empire Star.* Singapore.
W. S. WHEELER	Lamptrimmer	Bronze Medal	*Andalucia Star.* For saving life at sea.
L. WHITE	A.B.	B.E.M.	*Melbourne Star.* Survivor.
R. WHITE	Ch. Officer	D.S.C.	*Brisbane Star.* Malta Convoy.
R. WHITTON	Greaser	Desp.	Malta Convoy.
F. WILSON	Bosun	D.S.M.	*Brisbane Star.* Malta Convoy.
S. WILTSHIRE	Asst. Steward	Comm.	For services when *Imperial Star* bombed in port.
P. WINSOR	W/T Officer	M.B.E. Lloyds Medal	*Sultan Star.*

APPENDIX III
BLUE STAR LINE
WAR LOSSES

Arranged in chronological order   A/C.=Aircraft.   S/M.=Submarine.   T.=Torpedo.

Ship	Gross Tons	Date	Cause	Remarks
Ionic Star ..	5,602	17 Oct. 1939	Wrecked	Northern Ireland.
Doric Star ..	10,093	2 Dec. 1939	Sunk by raider	*Admiral Graf Spee.* 19° 15′ S. 5° 5′ E.
Sultan Star ..	12,306	14 Feb. 1940	S/M. T.	48° 54′ N. 10° 3′ W.
Adelaide Star	11,900	April, 1940	Captured	by Germans during occupation of Denmark.
Wellington Star	13,212	16 June, 1940	S/M. T.	42° 39′ N. 17° 1′ W.
Avelona Star..	13,375	30 June, 1940	S/M. T.	46° 46′ N. 12° 17′ W.
Arandora Star	15,500	2 July, 1940	S/M. T.	55° 20′ N. 10° 33′ W.
Auckland Star	13,212	28 July, 1940	S/M. T.	52° 17′ N. 12° 32′ W.
Napier Star ..	10,115	18 Dec., 1940	S/M. T.	58° 58′ N. 23° 13′ W.
Almeda Star..	14,934	17 Jan., 1941	S/M. T.	58° 16′ N. 13° 40′ W. Lost with all hands.
Afric Star ..	11,900	29 Jan., 1941	Raider	8° 0′ N. 25° 0′ W. (approx.).
Rodney Star ..	11,802	16 May, 1941	S/M. T.	5° 3′ N. 19° 2′ W.
Imperial Star..	12,427	27 Sept., 1941	A/C. T.	37° 31′ N. 10° 46′ E. Finally sunk by naval vessel.
Tacoma Star..	7,924	1 Feb., 1942	S/M. T.	37° 33′ N. 69° 21′ W. Lost with all hands.
Scottish Star ..	7,224	20 Feb., 1942	S/M. T.	13° 24′ N. 49° 36′ W.
Avila Star ..	14,443	5 July, 1942	S/M. T.	38° 4′ N. 22° 46′ W.
Viking Star ..	6,445	25 Aug., 1942	S/M. T.	6° 0′ N. 14° 0′ W. (approx.).
Tuscan Star ..	11,449	6 Sept., 1942	S/M. T.	1° 34′ N. 11° 39′ W.
Andalucia Star	14,942	6 Oct., 1942	S/M. T.	6° 38′ N. 15° 46′ W.
Empire Star ..	12,656	23 Oct., 1942	S/M. T.	48° 14′ N. 26° 22′ W.
Pacific Star ..	7,951	27 Oct., 1942	S/M. T.	29° 16′ N. 20° 57′ W.
Dunedin Star..	12,891	29 Nov., 1942	Wrecked	Ran ashore near Cape Frio, South West Africa. Total loss.
California Star	8,293	4 Mar., 1943	S/M. T.	42° 32′ N. 37° 20′ W.
Empire Lakeland ..	7,015	11 Mar., 1943	S/M. T.	Presumed torpedoed in 58° N. 15° W. (approx.). Lost with all hands.
Canadian Star	8,300	18 Mar., 1943	S/M. T.	53° 24′ N. 28° 34′ W.
Celtic Star ..	5,574	29 Mar., 1943	S/M. T.	4° 16′ N. 17° 44′ W.
Melbourne Star	12,805	2 April, 1943	S/M. T.	28° 5′ N. 57° 30′ W. (estimated).
Royal Star ..	7,900	20 April, 1944	A/C. T.	37° 2′ N. 3° 41′ E.
Empire Javelin	7,200	28 Dec., 1944	S/M. T.	50° 4′ N. 1° 0′ W.

A total of 29 ships lost, with a gross tonnage of 309,390

APPENDIX IV
BLUE STAR LINE
VESSELS THAT SURVIVED THE WAR

Albion Star	*Columbia Star*	*Norman Star*
Australia Star	*Fresno Star*	*Sydney Star*
Brisbane Star	*Gaelic Star*	*Trojan Star*
Britanica	*New Zealand Star*	*Tudor Star*

INDEX

Names of Blue Star ships are printed in small capitals.

Vian, Captain (R.N.) Philip ; 31—34.
Victorious, H.M.S. ; 90.
VIKING STAR ; 98—105.
Vincent, Able Seaman W. H. ; 156.
Waimarama, (S.S.) ; 93, 94.
Wairangi, (S.S.) ; 93.
Walker, H.M.S. ; 45.
Walsh, Capt. W. ; 47, 48.
Walton, F. ; 70.
Warspite, H.M.S. ; 80.
Wastwater, H.M.S. ; 142.
Watson, Ch. Off. M. C. ; 66.
Waugh, 4th Eng. H. ; 156.
Weller, 2nd Eng. H. G. G. ; 63.
WELLINGTON STAR ; 37, 38, 46.
Welshman, H.M.S. ; 79.
Westerwald, (German supply ship) ; 17.

Weston, Mr. (Purser) ; 67.
Wheeler, Lamptrimmer W. S. ; 108, 109.
White, Able Seaman L. ; 144, 145.
White, Ch. Off. R. ; 96.
Whitehead, Capt. R. G. ; 59.
Whitshed, H.M.S. ; 36.
Whitton, Greaser R. ; 96.
Williams, Capt. T. ; 38.
Wilson, Bosun F. ; 96.
Wilson, Capt. G. ; 81.
Wilson, Eng. R. ; 72.
Windsor, H.M.S. ; 39.
Winsor, W/T Off. P. G. ; 35, 37, 135.
Wolf, (German raider) ; 50.
Wright, Capt. G. (Singapore Pilot Service);
    62.